A BRIEF GUIDE TO

Cloud Computing

Christopher Barnatt

ROBINSON

Constable & Robinson Ltd
3 The Lanchesters
162 Fulham Palace Road
London W6 9ER
www.constablerobinson.com

First published in the UK by Robinson,
an imprint of Constable & Robinson Ltd, 2010

ISBN 978-1-84901-406-9

Printed in Great Britain by Clays Ltd, St Ives plc

Disclaimer
While every effort has been made to ensure that the content in this book is as
accurate as possible, no warranty or fitness is implied. The information is
provided on an 'as is' basis, and the author and the publisher take no
responsibility for any loss or damages arising from its use.

1 3 5 7 9 10 8 6 4 2

To Helen

CONTENTS

Acknowledgements   ix

Preface   xi

Part I: Cloud Computing Basics

Chapter 1   The Rise of Fluffy Computing   3

Chapter 2   Cloud Computing and Web 2.0   26

Chapter 3   Software in the Cloud   43

Chapter 4   Hardware in the Cloud   76

Part II: Cloud Computing Implications

Chapter 5   Security, Privacy and Reliability   107

Chapter 6   The Second Digital Revolution   127

Chapter 7   The Battle for the Cloud   150

Chapter 8   Trouble in the Boardroom   179

Chapter 9   The Personal Cloud   200

Chapter 10 Cloud Computing in the Future   215

Cloud Computing Directory   236

Glossary   249

Index   265

ACKNOWLEDGEMENTS

I would like to thank Leo Hollis for asking me to write this book and then editing it; Kate Pollard for managing the publication process; Richard Rosenfeld for his copy-editing; Mark Daintree for checking parts of the manuscript and helping me introduce others to the cloud; Thomas Chesney, Duncan Shaw and George Kuk for allowing me to bounce ideas around; my parents for their support as I embarked on the journey of yet another book; and Tabitha Browne for being Tabitha Browne.

PREFACE

Computing is facing another revolution. This time it is called 'cloud computing' and involves accessing software applications, data storage and processing power over the Internet.

Gaining access to computing resources online may not initially seem that radical a proposition. However, cloud computing is already starting to turn the software industry upside down. After all, once people start running programs over the Internet they will have no need to purchase and install them on their own computers. Companies will also not be required to purchase and maintain so much hardware and software if it can simply be rented online. The growth of cloud computing therefore threatens the survival of many software vendors and corporate data centres.

For most people cloud computing will be extremely liberating. This is because it will transform computing into an on-demand utility much like water or electricity. What this means is that, in the near future, computer power will simply be 'on tap' for us to consume as we please. The Internet already provides the infrastructure to allow this to happen. Pioneering cloud computing suppliers are also already peddling their highly cost-effective wares. All that is required is for more people to appreciate the benefits of not having to invest in computer hardware and software that is rarely fully utilized.

This guide to cloud computing comes in two parts. Part I introduces the basics and explains the advantages of cloud computing, its association with Web 2.0, and the range of online software applications and hardware resources already available. In short, Part I covers what anybody who wants an understanding of cloud computing really has to know about.

Part II provides a broader coverage of the implications of cloud computing, and the different chapters might interest some more than others. The topics covered include security, privacy and reliability, next generation cloud hardware, battles ahead in both the computing industry and many boardrooms, personal clouds, and a glimpse into the future. Come to think of it, every chapter ought to interest everybody!

This book is not a supplier showcase. However, with any technology development as new as cloud computing, it is impossible to explain what is going on without significant reference to actual product offerings. Throughout this book you will therefore find reviews of specific cloud computing services. Many of these are even free to use straight away just by visiting the web addresses included in the text.

Like it or loathe it, cloud computing is already starting to have a significant impact on the personal and corporate computing landscape. Within a decade it is also likely to be the only computing show in town. None of us can therefore ignore cloud computing. Our only real choice is whether we want to be part of the steamroller or part of the road.

Christopher Barnatt
Lecturer and Futurist
April 2010

A Special Note on Web Addresses

A great many web addresses are included in this book. Most appear in the text without a 'www' or 'http://' prefix – e.g. docs.google.com – and were checked at the time of publication to work in this format. However, a few web addresses are included with a 'www' prefix, for example www.itfarm.co.uk. When this is the case the 'www' part does need to typed into your web browser to access the site. Note that when a web address is included at the end of a sentence, the full stop does not form part of the address. Also note that links to the majority of web resources included in this book are featured in the Cloud Computing Directory on pages 236–48. This directory is also available online from **explainingcomputers.com/cloud**.

Part I

CLOUD COMPUTING BASICS

I

THE RISE OF FLUFFY COMPUTING

This book is being written in the cloud. This means that my word processor is not installed on my computer. The files for each chapter are also not being saved on one of my own hard disks or USB keys. Instead, the program I am using is running somewhere 'out there' on the Internet. My files are then being saved to remote online storage. This service is also being provided to me for free.

Exactly where my word processor is running and where my files are I really have no idea. More importantly, I simply don't care. This is also the whole point. Cloud computing is 'fluffy' because the resources being used are irrelevant to the vast majority of users. This is why cloud computing is so scary and resisted in many corporate data centres. It is also why cloud computing is so liberating and powerful for the rest of us.

Just before you think that I have no idea what I am doing, I can reveal that this book is being written in Google Docs. As illustrated in screenshot 1.1, this is an online word processing, spreadsheet, drawing and presentations package now being used by tens of millions of people and an increasing number of companies. In the UK, the *Daily Telegraph* and *Sunday Telegraph* national newspapers are now partially written in Google Docs. This has been occurring since July 2008 when the Telegraph Media Group began a transition from local Microsoft software to the online Google Apps software suite.

Jaguar Land Rover, Rentokil Initial and the District of Columbia government are just three of the far larger organizations that have also adopted Google Apps. Meanwhile universities from Arizona to Delhi, Washington to Notre Dame, and Dublin to Leeds, are in a stampede to sign up to Google Apps Education Edition. Strange and scary as it may initially seem, make no mistake that cloud computing is already entering the mainstream.

This book is your guide to the dawning age of cloud computing in which all manner of computing resources will be accessed over the Internet. It is therefore a book about a technological change as radical as the personal computer revolution. This is, however, not a technical tome. Rather, *A Brief Guide to Cloud Computing* is your route map to the future practices and philosophy of computing and how they will affect us all.

So What Exactly is the Cloud?

You may be wondering what any of this has to do with clouds! The answer is that, for many years, the Internet has been represented on network diagrams by a cloud symbol. When, around 2008, a variety of new services started to emerge that permitted computing resources to be accessed over the Internet, the label 'cloud computing' started to be used as an umbrella term. So does this mean that we ought to be talking about 'Internet computing'? Well, perhaps. However, in the strictest sense, the 'cloud' is a label for online computing resources rather than the entire Internet. The term 'cloud computing' is also useful because it distinguishes the kinds of things we have been doing online

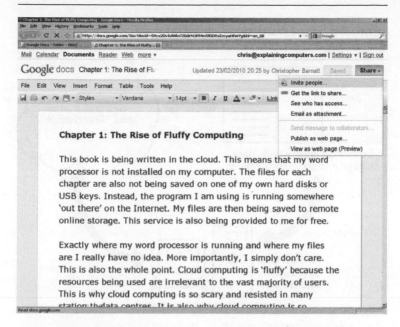

Screenshot 1.1: Word processing in Google Docs

for a couple of decades from a totally new age of online software and processing power.

Figure 1.1 illustrates the key differences between traditional and cloud computing. As shown in the top half of the figure, at present local software is installed and data is stored on most personal computers. Most computer users in organizations also access enterprise applications, data storage and processing power from a corporate data centre. The Internet may additionally be used and often relied upon. However, until now, for most people Internet usage has been confined to accessing information from websites and exchanging e-mails and file attachments.

The lower half of figure 1.1 shows the brave new world of cloud computing. Here the corporate data centre has been decommissioned. Also, software applications and data are

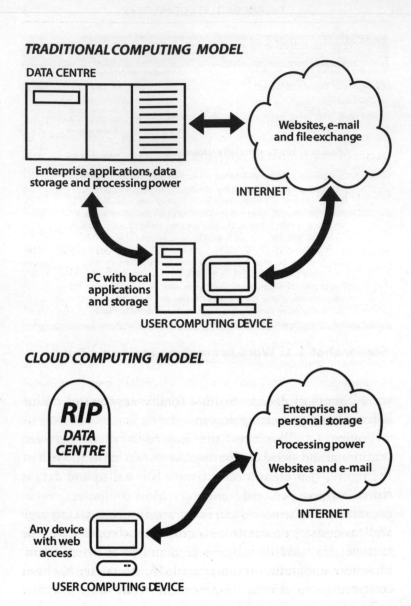

Figure 1.1: Traditional and cloud computing

no longer installed and stored on a user's computing device. Rather, enterprise applications, personal applications, data storage and remote processing power are all accessed from the cloud.

The scenarios shown in figure 1.1 indicate the two most extreme positions, with a hybrid model somewhere in between being most likely in the medium-term. Even so, the implications of ceasing to install all applications and store all data on personal computers or in a data centre will be very significant. Not least, as explored in chapter seven, there will be major ramifications for traditional software companies such as Microsoft. As discussed in chapter eight, the implications for those who currently work in company IT departments will also be just as great.

In practical terms, the cloud is made up loads of giant data centres – also known as 'server farms' – run by Google, Amazon, Microsoft, IBM, Apple and a host of other traditional and emerging computing giants. While the sorts of online services that can be offered from the cloud are quite varied, they can largely be classified under the two broad headings of 'online software' and 'online hardware'. Lots of information and examples to demonstrate what this means in practice are provided in chapters three and four respectively.

Killer Benefits
So why, you ask, would anybody want to cloud compute? Well, as figure 1.1 indicates, over time cloud computing will remove the need to install and maintain many local or corporate computing resources. In the shorter term, cloud computing also offers a couple of immediate killer benefits.

The first immediate benefit of cloud computing is that data and applications are accessible from any computer on the Internet. This book, for example, is being written in my home office, my university office and on an Eee PC netbook in all sorts of other interesting locations. By writing the book in a cloud word processor, I never have to worry whether the next computer on which I work will contain the most recent version of each chapter.

The second immediate advantage is that cloud computing is collaborative. I happen to be writing this book all by myself. However, if I had a co-author my cloud word processor would really come into its own, with each of us always being able to work on the latest version of any chapter, and even at the same time. Just in case this is getting you excited, I should point out that lots of information on collaborative working with specific cloud computing applications is provided in chapter three.

Text documents are also far from the only forms of data starting to take up residence in the cloud. Photographs, music, e-mail, personnel files, accounts, videos, books and more are already being manipulated over the Internet as cloud computing advances. As will be revealed throughout this book, whatever you do or want to do with a computer it is likely that there is already a suitable cloud computing application.

Alongside any-device access and collaborative working, cloud computing also has a number of wider benefits. As we will explore shortly, these include cloud computing being cheaper and more environmentally friendly than traditional computing. Online processing power and cloud data storage are also essential for the development of new computing applications like augmented reality.

Security, Privacy and Reliability

Before we get too evangelical, it has to be said that cloud computing does have its fair share of potential drawbacks. Most obviously, there is the dependence of any cloud computing application on a reliable Internet connection.

While for some this may present a problem, it nevertheless remains the case that a great many homes and most organizations do now have a reliable and high-speed Internet connection. Over the next few years, those that do not have one can probably expect connectivity to improve. Which brings us to most people's far bigger worry – security and privacy.

Many cloud computing concerns about security are likely to be perceptual rather than real. Anybody who sends an e-mail is already trusting the confidentiality of their material to their Internet service provider, not to mention all those companies who run the Internet infrastructure over which their message will travel. This means that any document written in, say, Microsoft Word and sent as an e-mail attachment is already no more secure and confidential than a document written in Google Docs or any other online word processor. To a large extent, when it comes to security and privacy, cloud computing developments simply highlight how trusting of the Internet we have already perhaps blindly become.

Security issues may also at least in part be accounted for contractually. For example, when in October 2009 Los Angeles City Council decided to move its 30,000 employees to Google's Government Cloud services it got a powerful security-breach penalty clause added to the contract.

For individuals and those working in smaller organizations, cloud computing is also likely to reduce their risk of security disasters. As YouTube user AnswerFortyTwox posted in response to a security-conscious viewer of one of my early cloud computing videos:

From the perspective of a hacker . . . it is infinitely easier for me to break through the meagre security on a personal computer than it is for me to take on a Google server. In a way, your documents are safer.

As further explored in chapter five, the benefits of cloud computing already outweigh the potential security, privacy and reliability drawbacks in the vast majority of cases. Stand-alone desktop and data centre computing may continue to prove essential for certain specialist types of users and applications. However, for the majority of us most of the time, cloud computing is the future.

Key Cloud Computing Characteristics

Given that it is fluffy by nature, it is quite difficult to provide a totally precise and widely accepted definition of cloud computing. This is partly because different technical computing specialists will opt for a different emphasis in their definitions than most end-users. After all, while for most people cloud computing is about simplifying things and masking complexity, for computing specialists it already involves new technologies and new career structures. You should therefore not expect a data centre manager, a programmer, a typical business computer user or a private individual to define cloud computing in precisely the same manner. This said, definitions do remain important.

I have already explained that cloud computing involves software applications, processing power and data storage being accessed online. Building on this, from most people's perspective we can also state that cloud computing is where dynamically scalable, device-independent and task-centric computing resources are obtained over the Internet, with any charges (where payable) being on a per-usage basis.

While the above is a somewhat long and involved definition, it does at least bring together in one sentence cloud computing's four key characteristics. I will also now explain these in more depth.

Cloud computing is dynamically scalable

Cloud computing is dynamically scalable because users only ever have to consume the amount that they actually want. Just as we are used to drawing as much or as little electricity as we need from the power grid, so any user can draw as many or as few computing resources from the cloud as they require at any particular moment. This means that individuals and organizations will no longer have to invest in computing resources that often sit idle. Nor will they have to wait in frustration for complex computing tasks to be completed due to a lack of available processing power.

One of the first major suppliers of dynamically scalable cloud computing resources was Amazon. Yes, the company that started out selling books online – though which in reality has always been a logistics business – is now selling computer-processing power by the hour. And I mean that quite literally. Via a service called Elastic Compute Cloud, or 'EC2', Amazon sells cloud computing processing capacity in what are termed 'instances'. As Amazon explain, EC2:

> ... allows you to obtain and configure capacity with minimal friction. It provides you with complete control of your computing resources and lets you run on Amazon's proven computing environment. Amazon EC2 reduces the time required to obtain and boot new server instances to minutes, allowing you to quickly scale capacity, both up and down, as your computing requirements change.

At the time of writing, the smallest standard Amazon EC2 instance is a 1.2GHz 32-bit virtual processor core with 1.7Gb of memory and 160Gb of storage. This can be provided running either Windows or Linux for around 5p an hour.

If the last two paragraphs sound like a load of technical gibberish, then please don't panic and just read on! The key point right now is that cloud computing developments like EC2 allow anybody to purchase any capacity of computer power they want both cheaply and on an hourly basis. Amazon EC2, its competitors, and their business implications, are discussed in chapter four.

Cloud computing is device-independent

I have already noted that cloud computing resources can be accessed from any computer on the Internet. It is, however, worth stressing that this does not just mean any computer, but any *kind* of computer. Provided that it has an Internet connection and a web browser, it really does not matter if the computer is a traditional desktop or laptop PC, or even a netbook, tablet, smartphone, e-book reader, surface computer, ambient device or any of the other new computing appliances discussed in chapter six.

Again, this is a radically new development. While over the past decade it has become easy to exchange data between different computers, this still requires the right software to be installed. For example, if a presentation is created in Microsoft PowerPoint and sent to somebody as an e-mail attachment, the recipient needs to have Microsoft PowerPoint on their computer to open and edit the file in a completely compatible manner. However, if the presentation is created in Google Docs then it can be opened and edited on any kind of computer with an Internet connection and a web browser. This even includes viewing and editing the presentation on some Internet-enabled mobile phones.

Device independency will be of increasing importance as more of us access the Internet using smartphones, tablets and other pocket and handheld devices. For many years, manufacturers have been building cut-down versions of Word, Excel and PowerPoint into mobile devices to allow us to access and work on documents on the move. However, this has very much been a second-best solution, with a lack of total compatibility between the desktop and mobile software versions. For anybody who wants to work on documents on a phone using exactly the same software that they use on a laptop or desktop, cloud computing is therefore already a Godsend.

Cloud computing is task-centric

Cloud computing is task-centric because the usage model is based entirely around what users want to achieve, rather than any particular software, hardware or network infrastructure. Users do not have to purchase or install anything before using a cloud computing resource. Nor do they have to maintain or pay for anything during periods in which no resources are being used.

As David Malcolm Surgient of ZDNet explains, cloud computing 'abstracts away' the traditional, infrastructure heavy view of pre-defined computing environments still maintained by most organizations. As David nicely puts it:

> In most cases, users of the cloud generally want to run some business service or application for a specific, timely purpose; they don't want to get bogged down in the system and network administration of the environment. They would prefer to quickly and easily access a dedicated instance of an application or service.

For many years Microsoft marketed its wares under the slogan, 'Where do you want to go today?' The answer was presumably that we wanted to go to a computer and install some Microsoft software that would, in turn, allow us to get on with what we actually wanted to do. Cloud computing cuts out the 'going to a computer and installing something' step. Rather, if you want somebody to see or edit a document you just send them a link.

The above means that cloud computing will allow us to simply get on with those many activities that involve a computer. Nobody today settles down to use a pencil. In contrast, lots of people do still consciously sit down to use a computer. Cloud developments may, however, start to catalyze a mentality shift from tool-in-hand to task-at-hand computer application.

Cloud computing has no fixed costs

In business, a fixed cost is something that has to be paid regardless of the number of people who use a certain facility or a company's level of production. A variable cost is different because it changes according to the number of people involved and output levels. For example, the annual cost of renting a factory is likely to be fixed. In contrast, the cost of staffing a factory, and of the raw materials it requires, will vary according to how much is produced.

Traditionally, computing has involved substantial fixed costs. Most significantly, these have included the cost of building, equipping and maintaining data centres. However, because cloud computing is dynamically scalable and task-centric, for most users it has no fixed costs. Rather, all costs are on a per-usage or variable basis. As demonstrated by the example of Amazon EC2, processing power can already be purchased from the cloud by the hour.

Software applications purchased from the cloud similarly incur only variable costs. Where provision is not free, charges are typically based on the number of people using an application each month, or the number of records or projects being worked on. So, for example, the online database software Zoho Creator is free for two users using up to three database applications. It then costs $15 per month for three users, $25 a month for up to five users, $45 a month for up to ten users, and so on – with the number of databases and records permitted also rising as the charge increases. As with Amazon EC2, the cost structure for Zoho Creator is also entirely elastic. This means that users are able to upgrade or downgrade their requirements at any time. A company with seasonal business can therefore license the software for a great many users only at their busy times of year.

The fact that cloud computing has only variable costs is extremely important for small companies. This is because small companies have not, until now, been able to afford the kinds of sophisticated business applications available to large corporations. However, because cloud computing suppliers such as Clarizen, Employease, Netsuite, Salesforce and Zoho do not charge an initial fixed-cost outlay, they are now levelling the software-access playing field. Indeed, as explained in chapter three, the latest types of human resource, project management, customer relationship management (CRM) and other applications can now be accessed from the cloud by any business, large or small.

The Only Show in Town
All of the basics of cloud computing have now been outlined. You may well think that everything expected of a first chapter has therefore been covered and that it is high time for chapter two. After all, you now know what cloud computing is, how it differs from current computing practice, what its key benefits and drawbacks may be, and hence why individuals and organizations may opt to cloud compute.

The above noted, what I have not familiarized you with yet are the broader reasons why we may all soon have to cloud compute. In other words, it is now time to explain why cloud computing will soon be the only mainstream computing show in town.

In October 2009, technology analysts Gartner cited cloud computing as the most strategic technology development for 2010, and hence a trend that no business can ignore. Their logic for this was complex and in part linked to everything discussed thus far. However, I would propose that cloud computing will become inevitable for the following three reasons:

- Cloud computing will be essential to remain competitive
- Cloud computing will be essential to be green, and
- Cloud computing will be essential for next-generation applications

I will now justify each of these rather bold claims.

The Competitive Cloud

We have already seen how cloud computing is dynamically scalable, task-centric and charged on a per-usage basis. As a consequence, cloud computing is likely to be more cost effective than current computing arrangements for most organizations. Indeed, the cost savings already speak for themselves.

The Telegraph Media Group, for example, expects to reduce its software costs by 80 per cent over three years following its switch from local Microsoft software to Google Apps. Some suppliers even claim cost savings of as much as 90 per cent. While such figures do need to be treated with some scepticism, there are nevertheless a great many companies – and especially small companies – with very positive stories to tell. US biotechnology pioneer Genentech, for example, claims savings of 'millions of dollars' from using Google and a range of other cloud computing providers. Not least this is because Genentech has avoided the construction of a new $10 million data centre.

In fact, the cost savings are potentially so great that in an increasing number of instances, cloud computing is likely to become the only competitively acceptable computing option. There is also a strong historical precedent for this. As explained by Nicholas Carr in his excellent book *The Big Switch*, around a century ago using electricity from a national grid – rather than generating it within a business – became a competitive necessity. This was simply because big electricity suppliers could leverage economies of scale that were unavailable to their customers.

Today the cloud is becoming the centralized power plant of the Information Age. In tandem, the mistrust being voiced by many in computing who do not want to use this new central utility service is also nothing new. As Carr notes, in 1900 there were about 3,600 public electricity-generating plants in the US, and yet around 50,000 private plants fuelling the energy needs of individual companies. Firms may have switched from water power to steam power to electricity. However, they still took some convincing to switch to an external electricity supplier. However, once convinced of the competitive necessity to switch they did not hesitate. For as Carr puts it:

By avoiding the purchase of pricey equipment, they reduced their own fixed costs and freed up capital for more productive purposes. They were also able to trim their corporate staffs, temper the risk of technological obsolescence and malfunction, and relieve their managers of a major distraction.

The above are today also the precise reasons that most companies will shift from internal to cloud computing. Cloud vendors are already able to reap very significant economies of scale by optimizing the use, support and upgrading of their infrastructure. For most companies, running computing internally will therefore soon be recognized as too costly a strategy except in very specialist situations. Developing a reliance on central resources is also not something to be feared. It was, after all, the centralization of food and water supplies that created civilization and permitted the rise and survival of the modern city.

As we go about our daily lives, few of us even consider our reliance on a wide variety of utility services and infrastructures beyond our individual control. If we do ever give them a thought, then I would suggest it is usually with thanks and relief that we do not have to individually forage and fight to gather the sustenance necessary to keep us alive. In a decade the same will apply when it comes to cloud computing – with even the idea that a typical organization should run its own data centre being unthinkable.

The Green Cloud
The second major factor that will force most of us to cloud compute will be the legal and moral requirement to use less energy and waste fewer resources. In other words, cloud computing will be essential to be green.

One reason why cloud computing is more environmentally friendly than in-house or desktop computing is because large external vendors can run their infrastructure highly efficiently. Cloud computing suppliers with hundreds of thousands of servers will rarely, if ever, need to have many machines powered while standing idle. In contrast, in most corporate data centres – let alone in smaller organizations – a great many servers and indeed desktop computers are kept running at well below full capacity most of the time. This means that electricity is constantly being wasted to power and cool under-utilized hardware.

Cloud computing vendors are already proclaiming their green credentials. Netsuite, for example, advertises that in 2008 its customers saved $61m in energy bills by using its web-based customer relationship management, accounting and other cloud applications. Whole countries are also waking up to the environmental potential of cloud computing. The Icelandic government, for example, has now recognized that in terms of carbon footprint, Iceland is one of the best places in the world to host large numbers of computer servers. With approximately half of the energy used by a large data centre going into cooling, putting cloud server farms in very cold countries also makes plenty of sense. This is because the cold air required to cool the computers can be drawn in from outside the data centre, rather than being chilled with electrical air-conditioning units. Iceland can also power its data centres with geothermal rather than fossil fuel electricity.

In preparation for its anticipated cloud computing 'cold rush', Iceland is laying high-capacity, fibre optic cables to connect the country with North America and Europe. Just outside the Icelandic capital Reykjavik, work is also well under way on one of the first of Iceland's massive cloud computing centres.

As Iceland is well aware, the world's data centres already have about the same carbon footprint as the airline industry. Computing is therefore going to come under significant pressure to be more environmentally friendly. The adoption of cloud computing can also help us achieve this in three important ways.

Firstly, as noted above, a move from in-house to cloud computing will allow large vendors to optimize the power usage of the servers on which we will all rely. Local server capacity will therefore no longer be powered but idle. We just have the significant hurdle of getting IT managers to stop server-hugging (which I address in chapter eight).

Secondly, if cloud computing is adopted then many individuals will be able to work on low-power computing devices that draw most of their computational capacity from the cloud. This means that over-specified personal computers will not be sitting on desks and drawing loads of power while they wait for their users to actually do something. Once again, the savings can be significant. The Canadian vendor ThinDesk, for example, has achieved energy reduction savings of up to 80 per cent for small and medium-size firms who have switched to low-power computers that rely on cloud services delivered from its TELUS data centre.

Thirdly, while a mass migration to the cloud will make computing less of an environmental problem, innovative cloud computing adoption may also make computing part of a broader green solution. Collaborative Internet tools are already enabling more people to reduce their business travel by teleworking from home at least some of the time. The more we cloud compute, the more we will therefore be able to take planes out of the sky and vehicles off the road. These broader implications of cloud computing are explored in more depth in chapter ten.

The Next Generation Cloud

The final factor that will make cloud computing essential is that many next-generation computer applications will only work in the cloud. Local software and data inevitably constrain collaboration and the anytime, anyplace, anywhere use of information resources. This means that we will be prevented from obtaining the benefits of new 'crowdsourcing' developments unless we cloud compute.

Crowdsourcing is where the Internet is used to help generate value from the activities of a great many people. Today, crowdsourcing mainly involves lots of people working together collaboratively to tackle a problem that in the past would have been left to just one individual or a small group. As will be discussed in chapter ten, we are therefore starting to see an increasing number of so-termed 'open source' developments where all of the involved intellectual property is created and shared online for mutual benefit. Already crowdsourced products and services in use or under development include computer software, robots, 3D printers, prosthetic limbs and electric cars.

An increasing uptake of cloud computing will make it easier for individuals to consciously work together on crowdsourcing projects. In addition, there is also a significant potential to crowdsource data not just from people, but also from things.

As will be discussed in chapter six, more and more everyday items – including fridges and even clothing – are now being given their own Internet connection. Using data from cameras and other sensors, smart cloud computing applications are also starting to recognize and monitor objects that do not have their own connection to the web. As these trends take hold and more objects directly or indirectly go online, we will start to witness the development of some quite innovative cloud computing applications.

For example, within a few years augmented reality will be commonplace. This will allow us to hold up a smartphone or other mobile device and see real-time data overlaid on the camera image shown on its display. When viewed on screen, buildings in the street or any product in a shop will be clickable if additional information is required. To allow this to happen, image recognition cloud applications will need to identify objects in view and associate them with GPS co-ordinates from our handsets and massive online databases. Sound unlikely? Well, as discussed in chapter six, first-generation augmented reality browsers are already on the market and running on some smartphones.

Pretty soon there will be so many cameras, microphones and other sensors online – at least in public spaces – that a great many objects will start to cast a constant 'data shadow'. While this may raise concerns, it will also allow us to reap crowdsourcing benefits similar to those of online social networking. Satellite navigation systems, for example, could advise on routes based not only on internal maps, but also the position and predicted intent of all other vehicles on the road. However, this will only happen if a great deal of data is pooled and shared in the cloud rather than being held and processed on local computing devices.

Future developments in artificial intelligence (AI) will probably also depend on crowdsourced data. Programming a mobile phone or a robot to recognize everything in view is likely to remain very difficult if internal data and processing power have to be relied on. On the other hand, a phone or robot with access to cloud resources including video feeds from other nearby cameras will be in a far better position to make sense of the world around it. This means that for computers to be usefully smart they will require access to information from our immediate environment that can only be crowdsourced from the cloud. In turn, along with augmented reality, the development of artificial intelligence is likely to be a very strong reason for the mass adoption of cloud computing.

*   *   *

Coming Full Circle?

Whenever I give a lecture or run a workshop on cloud computing, at least one person questions whether it is all basically just a return to computing's early days. After all, as they argue, in the 1960s and 1970s most computer users worked on 'dumb terminals' that were totally reliant on a connection to a mainframe or minicomputer housed in a remote data centre. Having cited this historical fact, they then argue that cloud computing is actually a very old idea and potentially a step backwards.

So is cloud computing bringing us full circle? Well the answer to this is a very definitive 'yes' and 'no'. On the 'yes' side, cloud computing will make most of the computing devices we use dependent on remote resources most of the time. This is, however, already commonplace and not something we should fear.

Mobile phones, for example, are computing devices that are pretty much useless without a connection to a 'cloud' infrastructure and this is readily accepted. Digital televisions are also complex computing devices that are totally dependent on an external data feed and this similarly does not make people worry.

While most people may not think of mobile phones and digital televisions as computers, these devices help us realize why cloud computing is quite distinct from the mainframe-and-dumb-terminal era. The key difference is that yesterday's dumb terminals were dependent on a very specific, small-scale computing infrastructure. In contrast, most cloud computing appliances will not depend on any specific local server or mainframe, or indeed on any dedicated local computing resource at all.

I have already explained how cloud computing is dynamic, device-independent and task-centric. We could also add that cloud computing is resilient. Granted, cloud computing will make us ever more dependent on remote computing resources. However, we must recognize that such remote resources are likely to be far better managed and less prone to failure than those in most internal IT departments. This is simply because the likes of Google, Amazon and IBM are able to specialize in running a great many data centres – what we can think of as large wisps of the cloud – and that scale plays a major role in the delivery of service continuity. If, for example, you were dependent on a constant electricity supply to stay alive, would you rather be connected to your own generator or an electricity grid fed by scores of power stations?

In late 2009, Google's Chief Executive Eric Schmidt stated that the cloud computing revolution will be bigger than the advent of personal computing. While he may be somewhat biased, I also tend to agree with him. The early years of the personal computing revolution may have briefly empowered individuals and freed many from the shackles of their IT department. Unfortunately, the network and Internet developments of the nineties and noughties then allowed IT staff to claw back into the corporate data centre a great deal of central control.

Within organizations, one of the great promises of the cloud is that it will turn computing into such a utility activity that it will never again be able to be centralized in-house. In the home, the cloud revolution is also destined to turn computers into on-off appliances that simply just work. To the future relief of so many, the days of ludicrously complex, misbehaving operating systems and corrupt or incompatible software will come to an end.

The IT function in many companies is today at a crossroads in the face of cloud computing developments that threaten to give users the kind of flexibility once briefly promised by personal computing and then cruelly snatched away. Battle lines are therefore being drawn not just in the computer industry, but within a great many companies. Small businesses are also being freed to compete on a level computing playing field, while environmental campaigners are becoming wise to online opportunities that can make computing more green.

The remaining chapters of this book will guide you through the aspects of cloud computing that everybody needs to know about and their associated implications. The content included is as current as it can be. However, exactly how the cloud computing revolution will unfold is inevitably at present unclear. This said, I think we can already be fairly certain that the computing landscape that the advancing cloud will leave in its wake will be very different from the one we know today.

2

CLOUD COMPUTING AND WEB 2.0

Some of the first things to take up residence in the cloud were human relationships. Indeed it was around twenty years ago that people started to post messages and share personal information in what were then termed virtual communities. Today, the descendants of these early online meeting places are called social networking sites. The most popular – Facebook – now also has around 400 million active users.

The fact that people have been socializing online for a couple of decades serves as a reminder that today's cloud computing revolution is not occurring in a vacuum. Rather, the trend to upload data and to link people and applications online has been growing steadily since the birth of the Internet. To fully understand cloud computing we therefore need to step back just a little to appreciate its broader context.

Unless you spent the years 1998 to 2000 living on the far side of the Moon (or perhaps at university) you are likely to have at least some recollection of the Dot Com boom and bust. In the late 1990s, careless investment in Internet ventures was taking place right, left and centre. However, claims that the laws of economics had fundamentally changed – and in particular that generating web traffic had become more important than making a profit – were to prove misguided. By March 2000 things finally came to a head and the speculative bubble of Dot Com mania burst.

In common with several previous technology-driven boom-bust cycles, the Dot Com bubble left a positive legacy in its wake. As had also happened following the construction of the canals and then the railways, after the folly of speculative over-investment ended a new communications infrastructure was in place. However, post Dot Com, there was also a significant risk that the potential of the Internet would be disregarded due to the financial folly of a relatively small minority.

Enter Web 2.0
While the First Internet Revolution was still trying to peel itself off the floor, the concept of Web 2.0 emerged. The term 'Web 2.0' was coined by Tim O'Reilly in 2004 to signal a second-coming of the Internet. Some still argue that Web 2.0 is no more than marketing hype. However, O'Reilly's intention was to find a label for the sorts of things that were proving successful online in the wake of the Dot Com collapse. In doing so, he was trying to signal that the Internet revolution was far from over. He was also hoping to indicate a positive way forward for our use of the web.

Defining exactly what is meant by Web 2.0 is about as difficult as nailing jelly to a wall. However, we can say with some certainty that Web 2.0 refers to the use of the Internet as a social tool and a service delivery mechanism. This means that Web 2.0 is concerned with establishing new or improved forms of online connection between people, between web-sites, or between people and software applications. Isolating these three possible types of online connection also allows us to identify the three key aspects of Web 2.0 as being:

- Interpersonal computing
- Web services, and
- Software as a service (SaaS)

Interpersonal computing is where two or more people communicate online. Web services is then where two or more websites are automatically interlinked. Finally software as a service is where people connect to online software applications. To help clarify these definitions, figure 2.1 illustrates the three key aspects of Web 2.0.

Each part of figure 2.1 shows two people with some websites floating between them in the cloud. At the top of the figure under 'interpersonal computing', the two people are linked mind-to-mind via a website, such as Facebook, MySpace or Twitter. In the 'web services' section, Web 2.0 developments are enabling two websites – and potentially two organizations – to interlink and automatically share information with no human involvement. Finally, at the bottom of the figure, we have 'software as a service'. This is where a person is linked to an application out in the cloud, such as the Google Docs word processor discussed in the last chapter.

An understanding of interpersonal computing, web services and software as a service will help you appreciate many of the cloud computing concepts, services and future developments discussed in later chapters. We will therefore now explore each of the three key aspects of Web 2.0 in turn.

Interpersonal Computing

During the 1980s and 1990s most computers were stand-alone devices used for solitary activities, such as word processing or playing games. However, we all know that today most computers are connected to the Internet and used as much for communication as for entirely individual

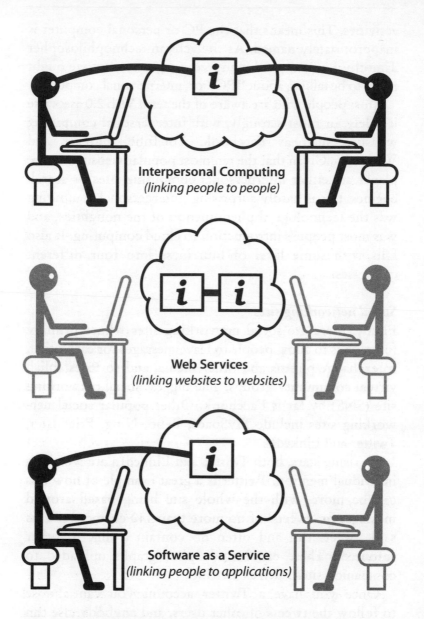

Interpersonal Computing
(linking people to people)

Web Services
(linking websites to websites)

Software as a Service
(linking people to applications)

Figure 2.1: The three aspects of Web 2.0

activities. This means that the PC or personal computer is inappropriately named. As the veteran technophilosopher Timothy Leary argued many years ago, by now we ought really to be talking about 'IPCs' or 'interpersonal computers'.

Most people who are aware of the term Web 2.0 associate it solely, or most strongly, with interpersonal computing websites such as Facebook, YouTube, Blogger and Wikipedia. Given that the ten most popular websites on the planet are either interpersonal computing sites or search engines, this is hardly surprising. Interpersonal computing was the technological phenomenon of the noughties, and was most people's introduction to cloud computing. It also falls with some level of blurriness into four different categories.

Social networking sites

Firstly, there are social networking sites whose primary function is to allow people to leave messages for each other, to exchange photos and other media, and so to establish virtual community groups. The biggest social networking site (SNS) by far is Facebook. Other popular social networking sites include MySpace, Bebo, Ning, Friendster, Twitter and LinkedIn.

As rising stars, both Twitter and LinkedIn are worth an individual mention. Twitter is a great example of how less can be more, with the whole site being based around messages or 'tweets' of no more than 140 characters. This said, tweets can and often do contain a link to other resources. These can include photographs uploaded to companion sites, such as TwitPic.

Once you have a Twitter account you can choose to follow the tweets of other users, and anybody else can follow you. You can also group those people you follow into lists to allow you to navigate through their tweets more easily. For example, you can group your tweets into 'personal' and 'business' categories.

LinkedIn is a business-oriented social networking site where users can log their professional profile including their career history, education and interests. By sending and accepting invitations, LinkedIn members form networks of connections. They can also advertise the sorts of communications that interest them. For example, a LinkedIn member may express an interest in consulting jobs, new ventures or certain areas of expertise. For those who use it wisely, LinkedIn is becoming a very powerful business networking tool.

Like all household-name social networking sites, Facebook, Twitter and LinkedIn are open to anybody and can be joined for free. However, social networking tools are now also starting to be used privately within companies in what is increasingly called 'Enterprise 2.0'. Many IT companies have launched online tools to which companies can subscribe if they want to build their own internal social networks. IBM, for example, offers a suite of social networking and online collaboration tools called LotusLive. Available from lotuslive.com, these allow employees to meet privately, share files, chat, manage projects and network online. The result, as IBM puts it, is that 'working together gets easier'.

Wikis

The second category of interpersonal computing site is the wiki. These are websites, or parts of them, that allow the collaborative authorship of documents. By far the most popular wiki is Wikipedia, the public, web-based encyclopaedia with over three million articles. Anybody can create or edit an article on Wikipedia, which is both its strength and its weakness.

Increasingly, private wikis are becoming popular in business as a means of running projects or replacing committees. Documents and questions can be posted for comment, with those in charge being able to decide who has the right to view and edit which documents. Anybody can now also create a public or private wiki in minutes using a free service, such as Zoho Wiki at wiki.zoho.com. Go on, have a go! You know you want to.

Blogs

Standing for 'web log', a blog is a chronological, journal-style website maintained by an individual in the form of an online diary. A whole host of websites enable anybody to start their own blog, with the best including Blogger and WordPress. A special blog search engine called Technorati currently tracks over 100 million blogs.

Video sharing

Last, but by no means least when it comes to interpersonal computing, are video-sharing websites including YouTube. While years ago the Internet turned anybody into a publisher, video-sharing websites serve as anybody's distributor. In other words, they provide everybody's online movie masterpiece with a chance of actually being found and watched.

YouTube and other video-sharing websites – such as Vimeo and DailyMotion – are powerful interpersonal computing tools because they allow everybody not just to add, but to augment and associate online video content. Adding content means actually uploading a new video (and preferably one that you have made yourself, rather than illegally stolen off the telly). This said, relatively few people upload video content, thereby making content augmentation and association in some ways more powerful.

Augmentation occurs when somebody registers on a site such as YouTube and rates an existing video or posts a comment on it. While augmentation does not involve an original creation, it is not as passive as just watching another person's upload. The discussions that surround some videos can even be as interesting as the videos themselves!

While relatively few users add or even augment content, everybody who uses an interpersonal computing website forges content associations. For example, when a YouTube visitor watches one video and then another, these two videos become associated. This means that the contents of the 'Related Videos' listing next to any video are directly influenced by what each visitor watches. Also driven by visitor viewing habits are YouTube's lists of featured and promoted videos, as well as its homepage content, such as those movies being 'watched right now'.

What content association very significantly highlights is how interpersonal computing is not just a conscious activity. The two minds interlinked at the top of figure 2.1 may never exchange a direct communication, such as a Facebook message or a tweet. However, the viewing decisions of one of these individuals can still directly influence the viewing activities of the other. In this way, the Web 2.0 phenomenon of interpersonal computing allows the cloud to become a mechanism for capturing what Tim O'Reilly calls 'collective intelligence'. In other words, the more we use interpersonal computing websites, the more the cloud is becoming an interlinked web of recorded human decisions that may guide us all.

All of this means that our online activities are increasingly being shaped by and shaping the actions of others. Which videos will you watch when you next visit YouTube? Simple. The recorded viewing habits of previous visitors will guide you to the most popular. This is why interpersonal

computing is so powerful. It is also yet another reason why
cloud computing will so radically change the computing and
information landscape.

The Rise of Web Services

While interpersonal computing is still getting all of the
attention, web services are where much of the Web 2.0 action
is currently at. Web services are online gadgets that
automatically exchange information between websites. So,
for example, if you visit a shopping site and click to pay by
Paypal, you end up interacting with two automatically
interlinked websites. The first is the one selling the goods,
while the second (Paypal) is the one that takes your money.
The fact that these two sites communicate automatically out
in the cloud is very clever indeed. However we hardly tend
to give it a thought and may not even realize that it is
happening.

Paypal is far from the only company to offer a web service
that can be plugged into another website like a piece of Lego.
Indeed, when it comes to taking payments online, many
shopping websites link behind the scenes to a payment
service provider or 'PSP', such as Netbanx or RBS
WorldPay. It is simply easier for most companies to plug in
a PSP web service than to muck about technically and
financially to set up their own online payment facility.

Anybody can now plug a PSP web service into their site
and start taking payments online in a matter of days or
even hours. For people who want to sell just a small range
of items, Google even offers the opportunity to add Google
Checkout 'buy now buttons' to any website. As
Google explains, these clever little buttons:

. . . will direct customers to a Google Checkout-hosted
purchase page where they complete their purchase with

Checkout. For digital goods, buyers will be able to download their order automatically once they complete payment.

The above signals the way in which web services are turning the construction of websites, and indeed businesses, into a plug-and-play activity. Plugging together services from different websites is now known as 'mashing'. Websites that draw their content from different services mashed together are then known as 'mashups'.

Alongside payment service providers, maps are now also very commonly mashed from one website into another. For example, look up a property on the estate agency website Rightmove.co.uk, and a map and local area information are embedded on the page. This web service is provided by AboutMyPlace.co.uk, to which the Rightmove site passes location information. AboutMyPlace in turn obtains the maps on to which it overlays local information from Microsoft Virtual Earth's Bing maps. When visitors view a property on Rightmove, they are therefore seeing a single web page mashed from three different service providers (RightMove, AboutMyPlace and Bing).

Many interpersonal computing websites also allow people to mash content. For example, a great many individuals and companies upload their videos to YouTube and then embed them back on their own website. This is easily done because once a video has been uploaded to YouTube the required embed web code is displayed by default (although users can opt to turn this off if they wish). The embed code can then be copied and pasted into another web page to make the video available there. Twitter also offers the facility to embed a feed of tweets into another website. This allows anybody to include a news feed on their website that they can update from anywhere just by posting a tweet.

Thousands upon thousands of web service gadgets are already available from the cloud. Many can also be mashed into other websites with little technical skill. As illustrated in screenshot 2.1, Google lists over 170,000 mashable gadgets on its Google Gadgets website, most of which have been programmed by third-party developers. Popular web service gadgets include calendars, games, currency converters, hotel and travel booking services, and some rather addictive virtual pets!

Two of my favourite web service gadgets are Sitepal and Google Translate. Sitepal allows anybody to add a photorealistic or cartoon-style talking character to a website, and is available from sitepal.com. While this is pretty cool, Google Translate is even more so, and is even free. Once embedded, Google Translate automatically allows visitors to translate a web page or even an entire site into over fifty different languages. This happens virtually instantly, and the first time you see it takes your breath away. It must also be worrying for professional translators. If you want to add Google Translate to your website, just go to translate.google.com and look under 'Tools and Resources'.

In the last chapter I indicated how cloud computing will be essential for next-generation computing applications. The growth of web services provides just one example of why this has to be the case. If individuals and organizations want to make use of the kind of 'embeddable functions' just described – let alone in development – then they have no choice but to embrace cloud computing.

Web 2.0 and Software as a Service

So far we have discussed how Web 2.0 developments can link people to people via interpersonal computing, and automatically link one website to another by creating a mashup of web services. The final aspect of Web 2.0 involves linking

Screenshot 2.1: Google Gadgets

people to computing resources, which in essence is what the remainder of this book is all about.

'Software as a service' or 'SaaS' is the technical term for a computer application that is accessed over the Internet instead of being installed on a computer or in a local data centre. Because the idea of people accessing software applications from the cloud was introduced in the last chapter – and because the whole of the next gargantuan chapter is devoted to online software applications – there is no reason for us to delve into the details of SaaS here. However, it is worth noting a couple of broad points in the specific content of Web 2.0.

Firstly, while it makes things easier to divide Web 2.0 developments into 'interpersonal computing', 'web services' and 'software as a service', there are overlaps between all three areas. For example, one of the reasons that companies are starting to use online office applications, such as Google Docs, is that they offer powerful collaborative facilities. In other words, some online software applications also function as interpersonal computing tools. As noted in the last chapter, in Google Docs it is possible for two or more people to work on a document, spreadsheet or presentation simultaneously. It is also possible to open up a real-time chat window concurrently with a document to allow its many authors to discuss what they are doing.

Secondly, it is also worth noting that many online software applications allow their output to be embedded into another website as a web service. For example, if a spreadsheet or chart is created in the free software application Zoho Sheet (sheet.zoho.com), it can then be embedded into any web page. This allows, for example, a pie-chart graphic on one website to be updated automatically every time the relevant data is changed in the Zoho Sheet cloud computing application. As another example, the sales figures in a private company wiki (possibly again hosted for free on Zoho) can be updated each time a salesperson enters data into the relevant Zoho Sheet spreadsheet, perhaps via their web-enabled mobile phone.

What I hope to have just demonstrated is why it is impossible to truly appreciate the power of software as a service without placing it in the context of interpersonal computing and web services. I also hope I am starting to show why ignoring cloud computing will place many individuals and businesses at a distinct disadvantage. OK, so now you probably just want to know more about software as a service! But please, stay with me and Web 2.0 for just another few pages. Patience is a virtue, or so they apparently used to say.

Web 2.0 and Cloud Computing Strategy

In the broadest sense, cloud computing is all about moving computing infrastructure online. The highly related developments of Web 2.0 then encapsulate some of the things that people use that infrastructure for. What this implies is that a successful Web 2.0 strategy ought to form part of any successful cloud computing strategy. This may perhaps sound rather obvious. However, the point is significant because many companies have yet to move beyond a strategy for their website, let alone the development of a broader Web 2.0 strategy and a clear vision for their uptake of cloud computing.

Today a good web strategy is as much about an effective use of cloud resources as it is about website design. As already noted, many Web 2.0 developments lead to the capture and exploitation of the collective intelligence of the many users of a website. It is indeed because websites like Facebook, Twitter and YouTube have become vast repositories of information and recorded human decisions that they are so popular. This popularity is also something that most businesses can take advantage of. A key part of any Web 2.0 strategy must therefore be to seek out where relevant collective intelligence has been pooled online and to establish a presence there.

Unfortunately, many companies still labour under the illusion that, when it comes to the Internet, all they need do is to create a nice website. Such a 'build-it-and-they-will-visit' approach effectively makes the assumption that customers will come to them. However, it makes far more sense to adopt a Web 2.0 strategy of inhabiting 'magnet' websites like Facebook, Twitter and YouTube. Such websites are where significant collective intelligence has already been pooled. By establishing a presence on these sites, a business is therefore making the sensible decision to actually go to its customers.

The majority of people visit one of a handful of popular interpersonal computing websites most times they go online. It is therefore crazy for any company not to set up shop where at least some of their potential online customers are actually known to be. A 'build-it-and-they-will-visit' Web 1.0 strategy is like waiting at home for people to knock on your door when you know that all of your friends and family are at a party across town. If you want to talk with these people then you must attend the party yourself.

Inhabiting magnet Web 2.0 sites is also not difficult. In fact, uploading videos to YouTube and then embedding them back on your own website as a web service is usually easier than hosting the video yourself. Not least this is because video hosting is YouTube's core business. Using YouTube or another popular Web 2.0 site to showcase yourself also significantly maximizes the chances of your online content actually being found.

It is very simple. For example, host a video solely on your own website and people only have a chance of seeing it if they choose to find and visit your site among millions. However, host a video on YouTube and its one hundred million visitors a month will also have the opportunity to find and watch your masterpiece. Anybody who finds, watches and enjoys your video on YouTube may then also click-on-through to visit the website of its creator.

To provide a practical example, the video content for my own ExplainingComputers.com website is hosted on YouTube. Of the first 200,000 views of these videos, around 93 per cent took place on YouTube itself, with only 7 per cent of people watching the videos on ExplainingComputers.com or other websites where they are embedded. About one third of the visitors to ExplainingComputers.com now also enter the site from its YouTube channel.

As I hope my personal experience demonstrates, using magnet Web 2.0 sites to capture visitors really does work. It just requires an acceptance that a successful online presence need not be entirely on your own website. As discussed in the first chapter, detaching yourself or your business from your own computing resources is what cloud computing is all about.

*   *   *

Towards Web as Platform

Web 2.0 pioneer Tim O'Reilly suggests that most Web 2.0 developments share two common characteristics. The first is their pooling of collective intelligence, while the second is what is known as 'web as platform'. We have already considered the implications of the pooling of collective intelligence on popular Web 2.0 sites like Twitter, Facebook and YouTube. I will therefore now bring this chapter to a close by examining O'Reilly's second Web 2.0 characteristic of 'web as platform'.

A platform is a framework for running things on. For example, Microsoft Windows is the most popular platform on which people currently run desktop computing applications. What 'web as platform' therefore means is that we will increasingly run things out in the cloud on the infrastructure of the Internet. As we have seen in this chapter, such things may be web services and software as a service. However, over time, the web will also become the platform on which we undertake an increasing proportion of our social and economic activities.

Web as platform is the concept at the very heart of cloud computing. It is also the idea that joins Web 2.0 and cloud computing at the hip. To a large extent Web 2.0 is a collective label for that increasing number of computing activities that could not exist without the platform of the web to run them on. In this sense, when it comes to cloud computing, Facebook, YouTube, Twitter, Wikipedia and their online kin have therefore shown us the way.

In particular, what popular Web 2.0 sites have demonstrated is the value of keeping information and applications not on our own computers but on a single, public computing infrastructure. The web is becoming to computers what the phone network has always been to phones. Imagine how useless a phone would be without a single, global network to connect it to. By the end of the decade, a computer without a connection to the cloud – to the platform of the Internet – is likely to have just as little value.

The Web 2.0 developments of the second half of the noughties have already shown us the kinds of applications – such as interpersonal computing, web services and software as a service – that will soon be the mainstay of cloud computing. However, perhaps even more significantly, the popular uptake of social networking and online video in particular have also begun to powerfully change attitudes towards computer use.

The hundreds of millions of people who today use social networking and online video sites have already begun to accept the value of storing information out in the cloud rather than on their own computers. Today's web service and SaaS pioneers have similarly let go of old ideas and have accepted a future in which most computing applications will be 'out there' in the cloud. Persuading more and more people to use and trust the cloud as their primary computing platform is without doubt the hardest challenge for advocates of cloud computing. However, what Web 2.0 developments have already shown is that most people can be persuaded to store and process data online once they are clear about the benefits that this may bring.

3

SOFTWARE IN THE CLOUD

This chapter is about software in the cloud. In other words, it is all about those word processors, spreadsheets, databases, presentation packages, photo and video editors, project management applications and far more that can now be run in a web browser.

As discussed in the last two chapters, software applications that are accessed over the Internet are known as 'software as a service' or 'SaaS'. Today SaaS is the most visible manifestation of cloud computing. It is also one of the most exciting and the easiest to understand.

SaaS applications have the advantage of being accessible from any device. This means that users can always access the most recent version of any document from their home PC, work PC, netbook, tablet or smartphone. Most SaaS applications are also collaborative. So, for example, two or more people can work on the same document at the same time, which makes remote working easier. In turn, it may even make our lifestyles greener by reducing our need to travel.

If you wish, you can read this chapter and immediately go to a computer and try out – for free – a wide range of very useful SaaS applications. In less than an hour online you can gain decent, practical experience of what cloud computing is all about and how it can benefit you or your organization. Remember the first time you used the world wide web? Well trying out SaaS for the first time is pretty much that magic-moment kind of computing experience.

Even though online software is a fairly new development, there are already far too many applications in the cloud to include all of them in this book. This chapter is therefore not a definitive guide to every SaaS offering. Rather, the intention is to showcase via selective examples the kinds of applications available in the cloud and how useful SaaS has already become. If, however, you do want to know about even more applications, you can turn to the Cloud Computing Directory starting on page 236 of this book. Alternatively you can search an online SaaS directory such as SaaSDir.com.

The New Software Frontier

In the second decade of the twenty-first century, SaaS has well and truly come of age. Having said this, it should be noted from the outset that many SaaS applications are less sophisticated than their locally installed counterparts. However, this is usually a blessing, as it means most SaaS applications are not overburdened with functionality that is not required by most users.

The vast majority of SaaS applications have been well written from scratch to simply get the job done. You may remember from chapter one that I described cloud computing as task-centric. Well, SaaS is certainly far more focused on what people actually want to achieve than many current mainstream software packages. Even Microsoft admits that most of us use less than 10 per cent of the functions in Microsoft Office.

Because SaaS applications are delivered over the Internet, they are continually updated. SaaS applications therefore do not have version numbers. Instead new functionality is constantly added incrementally.

When they first hear about constant updates, some people fear that they will make SaaS applications difficult to use. However, in practice the opposite is the case. This is because SaaS users never have to go through the upgrade hell often associated with a major revision and re-installation of a traditional software package. Rather, SaaS users simply find a new item added to a menu every now and again. Because SaaS is Web 2.0, most new functions are also the result of feature requests championed online by many other users.

All of the SaaS applications mentioned in this chapter will run on any kind of computer – PC, Mac, Linux netbook or whatever – providing that it has a broadband or other fast Internet connection. The only other requirement is a modern web browser. This specifically means Internet Explorer 8 or later, Firefox 3 or later, Apple's Safari 4 or later, or any version of Google Chrome. If you try many of the SaaS applications detailed below in earlier web browsers, they may not work at all. Even worse, and far more likely, they may only partially work. This would give you a poor impression of SaaS and could even drive you insane.

SaaS E-Mail

Lots of people now use a free online e-mail service, such as Google's Gmail, Yahoo! Mail or Windows Live Hotmail. Before these services existed, all e-mails were written in an e-mail application, such as Outlook Express, that was installed on the sender's computer. The message was then sent over the Internet and downloaded to the e-mail application installed on the recipient's computer. However, when e-mailing takes place between two people who use services like

Gmail, Yahoo! Mail or Hotmail, their messages never leave the cloud. The e-mail software used to write and read the message is also never installed on either user's PC.

As the above illustrates, those hundreds of millions of people who use web-based e-mail services are already quite happily using software in the cloud. E-mail is therefore the first major category of SaaS application. Cloud-based e-mail also looks likely to become as common in business as it already is in our personal lives.

For many organizations, e-mail is a relative no-brainer to outsource to an external supplier. This is because running e-mail servers is a generic computing activity that can involve significant administration costs. The security concerns that currently curtail the broader uptake of cloud computing in many companies are also less of a worry when it comes to e-mail. This is because all external e-mail messages are destined to end up in the cloud anyway. It is therefore difficult for even the most server-hugging IT department to argue against using SaaS e-mail.

As explored in the next section, major SaaS office suites, such as Google Apps and Zoho Business, already include web-based e-mail as standard. Their offerings are also proving increasingly popular, with other big players now entering the market.

To provide just one highly significant example, in October 2009 IBM waded into the cloud computing e-mail market-place with an SaaS offering called LotusLive iNotes. For $36 per user a year, this provides web-based e-mail and calendar functions. It also integrates with IBM's broader LotusLive suite of business social networking and collaboration tools mentioned in the last chapter. You can find out more at lotuslive.com.

As e-mail becomes cloud-based, it may evolve and integrate with other types of SaaS application. Google, for example, is currently trying to reinvent e-mail with a cunning SaaS offering called Google Wave. This is described by Google as an 'online tool for real-time communication and collaboration'. In effect, Google Wave is intended to be what e-mail would have been had it had been invented in the Web 2.0 Age.

Each Google Wave communication is 'in equal parts conversation and document', with the application allowing people to communicate and work together with richly formatted text, images, videos and more. Basically, think of each Google Wave communication as a widely sharable e-mail message in which any attachments are always editable and open.

In addition to its Wave offering, Google is also trying to reinvent e-mail by integrating social networking functionality. This has been achieved by adding an application called Google Buzz into Gmail. However, to date reviews of Buzz have been somewhat mixed. Not least much poor press followed Google's initial decision to configure Buzz to automatically follow everybody that a user most frequently e-mails. By default, this list of contacts was also made public and shared to all other followers. As we will discuss further in chapter nine, while Google's intention was to ensure that everybody had some online friends, the move inevitably raised serious privacy concerns.

Office SaaS

Apart from web-based e-mail, today most people have probably not used any other form of SaaS. However, almost every computer user will have some experience of a traditional office application such as a word processor or a spreadsheet. For most individuals or organizations, the best kind of SaaS application to start experimenting with is therefore a cloud-based office package.

All of the office SaaS applications covered in this section are very easy to use. Unless otherwise stated, they can also all be used for free, and most indefinitely so. New users just need to create an account by supplying a username and setting a password. All that is then required is to click on a link in a verification e-mail to complete the registration process. It is all very simple and painless.

It is worth noting from the outset that all of the following office SaaS applications are Microsoft Office compatible. In other words, documents can easily be exchanged with Microsoft Word, Excel or PowerPoint. To be absolutely clear, existing files can easily be uploaded to all of these online packages. Documents created or edited in them can then be downloaded out of the cloud to load into Word, Excel or PowerPoint. Some document formatting may be lost in the upload process. However, this minor niggle aside, there is no catch with any of the following. Honest!

Google Docs

Google Docs is the world's most popular online office application, and can be found at docs.google.com. The suite consists of a word processor, spreadsheet, PowerPoint-style presentation application and a drawing package. This is then coupled with an online storage service that allows users to upload, store, download and share any type of file. While most people currently use Google Docs for free, it is also one component of the for-a-fee Google Apps suite detailed in the next section.

Like just about every other SaaS office application, Google Docs is collaborative. By default, every document or file is private and can only be seen and edited by its creator. However, by using the 'share' menu, it is a simple matter to set any document so that it can be viewed or edited by others. Users can also send invitations to share their documents via e-mail links, as well as making entire folders of documents and uploaded files sharable. There is even the facility to send a link to a Google Docs document, or any other uploaded file, to somebody who does not even use the package.

The collaborative features of Google Docs really are incredibly useful. For example, they make it far easier for several people to work on the same report or presentation, or to update information, such as sales figures in a single spreadsheet. Rather than e-mailing around attachments for some poor sod to collate, everybody can work on the same document and everybody always sees the latest information.

The collaboration tools in Google Docs have been implemented with particular care. For example, in shared spreadsheets the cell or cells being worked on by another user are locked and highlighted in another colour. A chat window can also be opened up beside a shared spreadsheet to allow different users to discuss their changes in real-time. Some companies used to pay a small fortune for this type of specialist functionality!

Every time a user logs in to Google Docs they are presented with a file manager screen like that shown in screenshot 3.1. From here they can upload files, create and navigate folders, arrange files within them, and open existing documents. For example, clicking on a word processor document will open it up as previously shown in screenshot 1.1 on page 5. All of the expected text-formatting tools and menus are there just like they are in any other word processor.

From the main Google Docs screen, users can create a new word processor document, spreadsheet, presentation, drawing, form or folder. All are self-explanatory, apart from Google Docs forms. These are basically spreadsheet data entry screens that can be shared privately or publicly, or even embedded into other web pages. This makes, for example, conducting online surveys really easy. Users just create a new form, select a template from the scores available, and add their questions.

Screenshot 3.2 shows a simple Google Docs form created in under a minute. Every time anybody completes the form, a spreadsheet that Google Docs automatically creates is updated with the results in real-time. The spreadsheet for the form illustrated in screenshot 3.2 is shown in screenshot 3.3.

As I hope the above has started to signal, while Google Docs can simply be used as a free, collaborate online office suite, the potential is far greater. The Google Docs spreadsheet in particular can control a great many online things, and is therefore well worth becoming acquainted with.

As another example, anybody who wants to add an online store to their website can do so by embedding the Google Checkout gadget mentioned in the last chapter. They can then administer their store – adding and deleting products, changing prices and so on – simply by editing the Google Docs spreadsheet that Google Checkout automatically creates for this purpose. No programming knowledge whatsoever is required. (If you skipped chapter two on Web 2.0, you may want to go back and read the section on web services starting on page 34 to fully understand what I am going on about here.)

Google has done its homework with Google Docs. The functionality is not as sophisticated as Microsoft Office, but what most people need is there and works well. To make life really easy there are also thousands of templates available. These cover everything from household budgeting and invoices, to résumés (CVs) and business cards. Because Google Docs is a Web 2.0 tool, anybody can create a

Screenshot 3.1: The Google Docs file manager

template not just for personal use, but to instantly share with the world.

Learning to use Google Docs is easy if you can use a web browser and are familiar with a word processor, spreadsheet, drawing package or PowerPoint. There are also loads of Google Docs tutorial videos out there on YouTube and elsewhere in the cloud. However, a final specific feature worth mentioning here is the online file storage system that was integrated into Google Docs in early 2010.

Anybody with a Google Docs account can use the application to store any kind of digital data in the cloud, with 1Gb of file storage provided for free. If more storage space is needed, then each additional 20Gb costs $5 a year. Files that are not word processor documents, spreadsheets or

Screenshot 3.2: A Google Docs form

presentations cannot be edited. However, pdfs and most image files – including jpeg photos – can be viewed and printed. The fact that uploaded files and entire folders can easily be shared is also incredibly useful for those who need to exchange large files that are too big to attach to regular e-mail messages. Files can be uploaded up to 1Gb in size, which is fine for even fairly large videos.

Google Apps

I say, I say, I say. What do you get if you take Google Docs and bundle it with Gmail, Google Calendar, Google Video private video hosting, the Google Sites website and intranet creation tool, loads of storage space, and sell it for $50 per user a year? The answer is that you get Google Apps! This

Screenshot 3.3: The Google Docs spreadsheet linked to the form shown opposite in screenshot 3.2

may not be amusing. However, it is a line with punch given that over two million companies now run Google Apps, some of them with tens of thousands of employees.

According to Google and the many customers it parades on the Google Apps website, by switching from Microsoft Exchange e-mail and Microsoft Office to Google Apps, businesses can reduce their e-mail and office application IT costs by at least two-thirds. This is due to savings incurred in software licensing, running internal e-mail and other servers, and reductions in IT support staff.

Switching to Google Apps – as with any other SaaS application – also makes all IT costs known and variable. There are also far more opportunities for employees to work collaboratively after they have switched to SaaS.

Furthermore, by moving to Google Apps, companies give their employees what Google claims is fifty times the e-mail storage space (25Gb) than the industry average.

While anybody can use Google Docs, Gmail, Google Sites, Google Calendar and so on for free, purchasing them in the form of Google Apps provides the reassurance of 24/7 phone and e-mail support. Users are also exempt from the word processor, spreadsheet and presentation file storage constraints of the free version of Google Docs. At the time of writing these were limited to an upload file size of 500Kb for a word processor file (excluding any embedded images), 1Mb for spreadsheets and 10Mb for presentation files.

For non-commercial organizations, Google also provides educational, government and non-profit versions of Google Apps. To find out more go to apps.google.com. And please note that I do not have shares in Google, work for Google, or even earn a commission!

Zoho

Having told you all about Google Docs and Google Apps, Zoho.com is also an excellent place to start for anybody new to SaaS. As illustrated in screenshot 3.4, the company offers a wide range of office and collaboration applications, as well as some very powerful online business packages. Zoho does not have the mighty Google brand to promote its online wares. However, its products are excellent. In particular, Zoho's collaboration tools are every bit as good as Google's, as are the opportunities to share and embed document content via web links or across other websites as web services. You can even log in to Zoho using your Google username and password.

The Economist has described Zoho as 'the most comprehensive suite of web-based programs for small businesses'. It is also easy to see why. While the applications can sometimes be a little more sluggish than those in Google Docs, the range of functions is greater. For example, the page layout tools in the Zoho Writer word processor are better than in Google Docs. Zoho Writer also has a neat tabbed interface, though this can also be seen as a drawback if you are working on a small screen such as that on a netbook or tablet.

Where Zoho beats all of its competitors hands-down is with the sheer breadth of its offering. At the time of writing there were over twenty core applications, plus a range of utilities and plug-ins. Zoho is therefore the only SaaS provider listed here under both the 'office' and 'business' SaaS categories.

Alongside the Zoho Writer word processor, Zoho offers office workers its Sheet spreadsheet and the Zoho Show PowerPoint-clone presentation tool. There are also nice planner and chat tools, as well as an online document manager. The latter is called Zoho Docs (which can be somewhat confusing when Google Docs is an online word processor) and integrates with Zoho Writer, Sheet and Show. Zoho Docs also allows any type of file to be uploaded, stored and shared in the cloud.

A real killer application is Zoho Notebook, available from notebook.zoho.com. As shown in screenshot 3.5, this is a bit like a cloud scrapbook. Users are presented with a tabbed notebook of initially blank pages. On these they can then place and move around text, notes and any drawings they are able to scrawl. Other media can also be added, including video, directly dictated notes and other audio, images, web links, Zoho Writer or Zoho Sheet documents, or any other kind of uploaded file. As I said, it really is like a scrapbook in the cloud.

Zoho Notebook is very handy because you can just plonk down and move around virtually any kind of digital content.

Screenshot 3.4: SaaS applications available from Zoho.com

By dividing your digital cuttings into different notebooks made up of as many pages as you like, you can also keep all your digital collages highly organized and accessible from any computer. Notebooks or pages thereof can also be shared privately with selected individuals, or published for public web access. If you are the sort of person who does a lot of research – or indeed who just keeps coming across lots of potentially useful things as you roam the Internet – then

Zoho Notebook may well be just what you need to sort out your digital life.

In addition to a word processor, spreadsheet and presentation package, the professional version of most traditional office suites also contains a database application. While Google Docs does not feature one, Zoho has several. These include the highly popular Zoho Creator, which can be used to create just about any kind of online database. There are then several task-specific database applications for activities including invoicing and personnel management. These are detailed under 'SaaS Business Applications' on page 66.

Like Google, Zoho brings together its office applications in a paid suite. This is called Zoho Business and includes e-mail hosting, messaging, a calendar and the office applications outlined above. However, unlike Google Apps, Zoho Business is free for a company's first ten users. Additional users are then charged at $5 per user a month. This means that a business with ten or fewer employees can obtain all of the communications and office software it requires from Zoho for free.

Acrobat.com
OK, so you may have read this heading and thought Acrobat was a program for making pdf files? Or maybe somebody who performs daring feats in a circus? Well both of these are true. However, Acrobat.com is where you can find a suite of SaaS services and applications from Adobe. There is an online pdf creator for sure. However, you will also find cloud-based file sharing and storage, a very powerful web conferencing tool called ConnectNow, and a SaaS word processor, presentations package and spreadsheet named Buzzword, Presentations and Tables respectively.

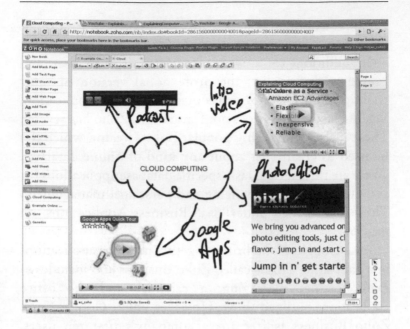

Screenshot 3.5: A page in Zoho Notebook

All of the Acrobat.com applications are extremely stylish with lots of cool animations. However, this does mean that they sometimes respond rather sluggishly if you do not have a fast Internet connection. That said, Acrobat.com's functionality is very good and there are also some excellent integrated tutorials. In particular, as soon as you have created an account you can access a document called *10 Cool Things You Can Do with Acrobat.com*. This provides a great overview of the package and its applications, and is a fantastic brochure for anybody to print out and use in their business to help make the case for adopting SaaS.

Because of the functionality available in the ConnectNow online meeting application, Acrobat.com is a potentially good choice for businesses who want a highly integrated

SaaS communications and office suite. With ConnectNow users can share all or part of their screens (which is just amazing!), as well as making use of online whiteboards, shared notes and online chat. In addition to collaborative file sharing, web-based audio or videoconferencing is also included.

While anybody can register to use Acrobat.com, under the free plan only five pdf files can be created and web conferences are limited to three people. There is then a 'Basic Premium' plan costing $14.99 per user a month that removes the pdf creation restriction, allows five people to meet online, and adds web and phone support. Prices then rise up to a maximum of $39 per user a month for a 'Premium Plus' plan allowing twenty-person web meetings. Given that Google Apps costs $50 per user a year and Zoho Business $5 per user a month ($60/year), the paid version of Acrobat.com is therefore somewhat expensive.

Microsoft Office Web Apps

In the summer of 2010, Microsoft launched Office 2010. In most respects this was simply the fourteenth version of the world's most popular traditional office suite. However, a new feature was Office Web Apps. These are free, web-based versions of Microsoft Word, Excel, PowerPoint and OneNote. However, they are not quite as straightforward or as flexible as the cloud office applications available from Google, Zoho and Adobe.

For some time Microsoft has offered a set of online services called Windows Live. One of these has been Office Live Workspace. This allows anybody to store and share files in the cloud, with office documents viewable in a web browser on any computer. However, users need to install on every computer they use the traditional Microsoft Office programs and a free plug-in called Office Live Update in order to create or edit documents. Compared to the online editing and collaborative functions available in Google Docs and other online office suites, Office Live Workspace has therefore been about as SaaS as a brick.

Office Web Apps are intended to replace Office Live Workspace and are major leap forward. However, at least at launch, Office Web Apps were not a direct online alternative to a locally installed version of Microsoft Office. Given that Microsoft still wants us all to purchase and install its desktop software, this is hardly a surprise.

Consumers can access an advertising-supported version of Office Web Apps for free as part of Windows Live. However, business users have to install Office 2010 before they can obtain all Office Web Apps functionality. This then allows them to access and share their documents from any PC or laptop computer, or any mobile device running Microsoft Office Mobile 2010. In effect, Microsoft's strategy has been to integrate online storage and its benefits into its traditional desktop and mobile office software.

Because Microsoft Web Apps are a companion to, rather than a replacement for, a locally installed version of Microsoft Office, the functions provided are inevitably somewhat limited. For example, while the Web Apps version of Excel allows simultaneous viewing and editing by multiple users, this feature is not included in the Web Apps version of Word. Microsoft also currently has no plans to provide it. The Web Apps version of Word is therefore not a true competitor to Google Docs, Zoho Writer or Adobe Buzzword if you want fully collaborative word processing.

On the positive side, Office Web Apps does manage to handle uploaded documents with 'full fidelity'. In other words, sophisticated formatting is not lost when documents are viewed or edited online, which does happen when complex documents are uploaded to Google Docs and other

SaaS word processors. Users of Office Web Apps are also provided with 25Gb of online storage for free.

SlideRocket

Fed up with full online office suites? Well so am I. Thankfully for us both then, SlideRocket is an online presentation package. Intended for very serious presenters, it is Microsoft PowerPoint compatible and far more sophisticated than any of its SaaS competitors.

SlideRocket presentations can include full-motion video and even integrate live data fed from, for example, a Google Docs spreadsheet. There is also the SlideRocket Marketplace where users can buy presentation themes, stock photography, cartoons, data feeds, videos, illustrations and more. These can then be placed in a personal presentation library for use when needed. In the SlideRocket Marketplace users can also buy graphic design, copy-editing, presentation coaching and other services. It is all exceedingly professional.

A thirty-day free trail is available at sliderocket.com. After that it is possible to continue to use all the basic tools for free (subject to a 250Mb file storage limit). However, it costs $12 per user a month for individuals – or $24 per user a month for businesses – to continue to access the most sophisticated functions.

SaaS Desktops

All of the SaaS applications mentioned so far run individually in their own browser window or tab. Suppliers, such as Google and Zoho, also offer really powerful cross-application integration and the ability to embed content from their SaaS applications into other web pages. Such an approach is also likely to be the future of office SaaS. However, it is not the only way that a suite of SaaS applications can be made available.

A few companies now deliver not just SaaS applications, but a cloud-based operating system and a desktop on which to run them. Some have even installed their cloud desktops with traditional non-SaaS office applications. Most analysts do not expect these kinds of SaaS offerings to gain any significant market share. However, just to provide a flavour, here are three of the best from the ten SaaS desktops currently available.

StartForce

Available from startforce.com, StartForce provides a Windows-like desktop or 'WebTop' loaded with a word processor, spreadsheet, presentations package and other applications. At the time of writing these include a pdf reader, contact manager, media player and messaging application. There are also various administration tools and a bulk file uploader for shifting lots of documents into the cloud in one go. Anybody can try StartForce without even registering. This is exactly what I did in screenshot 3.6.

EyeOS

EyeOS is an open source SaaS desktop. In other words, EyeOS has been written by a group of rather nice people for the goodness of humanity and not for commercial gain. (I will say more about open source and cloud computing in chapter ten.) EyeOS has a very clean interface with a top menu from which its users can launch a range of applications including a word processor, spreadsheet, calendar and presentation package. There is even a chess game if you want your computer to make you feel inferior. You can create an account to run EyeOS at eyeos.info, though it is also possible to install EyeOS on an internal server. To find out about the latter, to become involved with

Screenshot 3.6: The StartForce SaaS desktop

EyeOS development, or simply to find out more before creating a free account, point your browser at eyeos.org.

IT Farm

The clever chaps at IT Farm provide a paid service where standard Microsoft Office and other Windows packages are installed on their servers and delivered via a web browser. In effect, it is like running a cloud-based copy of Windows, which kind of makes you wonder why Microsoft is not offering this service.

By using the IT Farm, a company can potentially get rid of its own servers, and the IT support needed to run them, without having to change its office applications. For some businesses this may be an attractive way to embrace the cloud. While the service cannot be used for free, you can watch a video and try a demo at www.itfarm.co.uk. (Please note that for once you do have to type the 'www' into your address bar.)

SaaS Photo and Video-Editing

OK, with office SaaS and related desktops out of the way, we can now turn our attention to more visually creative tools. As I am sure you are aware – and as will be explored in chapter nine on the personal cloud – there are lots of websites that allow the storage and sharing of photos and videos. It is therefore worth stressing that what I am going to cover in this section are not websites like Flickr or TwitPic that simply allow their users to upload and share. Rather, here we are concerned with online applications that actually enable the creation and editing of visual media.

Photoshop Express

Have a look at photoshop.com and you will discover an online version of the industry-standard Photoshop image editing package. You can register for free – or just take a test drive – to discover the delights of online libraries and galleries that can be shared with your friends. However, from an SaaS perspective, the important thing is that you can also click on an image and select the 'edit' icon to do things like cropping, resizing, and making colour adjustments. Having said this, that is about all you can do.

I happen to be a die-hard Photoshop fan who spends a reasonable proportion of their life in the full, non-cloud version of the package. I am therefore rather sad to report that Photoshop's online cousin is very disappointing. This is not because it is no good at all. However, as we will shortly see below, while it is nice to discover Photoshop online, other SaaS image editors are just so much better.

Pixlr

Pixlr is my and many other reviewers' favourite online image editor. You can also go to pixlr.com and start using the package without even having to register. Once the Pixlr editor is running, an image can be created from scratch, opened from a local drive, or uploaded from anywhere on the Internet.

In contrast to Photoshop Express, Pixlr actually looks and behaves like the traditional full version of Photoshop running in a web browser. There are a wide range of image manipulation tools, plus a very wide range of filters that preview in real-time. There is even a history panel for undoing changes, as well as the ability to work on an image separated into layers. For those not used to such complex image-editing controls, a simpler, novice-friendly interface called Pixlr Express is also included.

Once you have finished working in Pixlr you have to save your image back to the computer you are working in jpeg, bmp, png or Pixlr's own PXD format. OK, so this means that images cannot be stored in the cloud. However, as an SaaS image editing tool, Pixlr is just so incredibly handy and really has no equal. If you are ever on a computer, need to edit an image, but do not have Photoshop or similar installed, then Pixlr is a godsend.

FotoFlexer

FotoFlexer describes itself as 'the world's most advanced online image editor'. The package certainly offers great integration with Facebook, Flickr, MySpace and other popular Web 2.0 sites. It also has a very clean, easy-to-use interface. However, the functions – while far greater than PhotoShop Express – are not quite up to the standard found on Pixlr. You can access FotoFlexer at fotoflexer.com.

When it comes to choosing an SaaS image editor it really depends on your individual requirements. If you want something that is dead-easy-to-use with cheery menus labelled things like 'beautify' (and another labelled 'Geek' where all of the real tools are) then you will love FotoFlexer. However, if you would rather have raw image manipulation power without the gimmicks, then Pixlr is a better bet. This said, with Pixlr you will have to store your final images somewhere else.

Jaycut

Just to prove that virtually any type of software application is now available in the cloud, I thought I should introduce you to the Jaycut online video editor. Yes, you read that right. Jaycut is an SaaS application that allows its users to upload video clips, drag them on to a two-track timeline, add titles, apply transitions and effects, and otherwise edit a movie. Wow! All in a web browser! Absolutely amazing.

Screenshot 3.7 illustrates Jaycut in action, but if you want to have a go yourself you can also find the package waiting patiently for you at jaycut.com. Granted, it is occasionally a little sluggish, but then so are many video-editing applications on most non-professional video-editing PCs.

Jaycut is a great example of the fact that SaaS no longer has any functional limits. For the YouTube generation, Jaycut therefore has to be where SaaS is currently at.

SaaS Business Applications

We have now waded through so much online software that it may have gone over the top of your wellies! If you only want to use SaaS at home, we may also by now have covered everything you need or want to know about. However, if you are running a business, or thinking of running a business – or want somebody to use SaaS to help run the business you

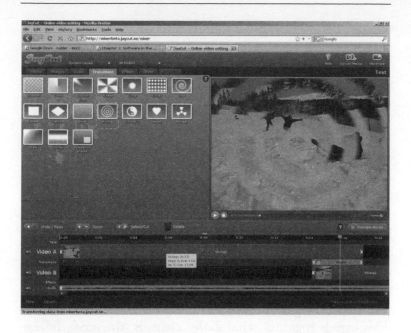

Screenshot 3.7: The Jaycut online video editor

work for better – then please continue with the rest of this chapter. Go on, pull on some taller waterproof boots, and we will take the plunge into a sea of just a few of those SaaS applications written specifically for business purposes.

Zoho

Earlier in this chapter I introduced Zoho as a quality provider of cloud office applications. Well, as noted a few pages back, Zoho also has the distinction of supplying a wide variety of other business applications. Just flick back to screenshot 3.4 on page 56, to see the range of goodies it has on offer in the cloud.

Zoho's most popular business software application is Zoho Creator. Available from creator.zoho.com, this allows custom database applications to be built online. To some extent, Zoho Creator can be thought of as a web-based version of Microsoft Access. However, as it runs in the cloud, Zoho Creator is in many respects more powerful because it offers the ability to create online databases that can be used simultaneously by many of a company's employees or customers. These databases can also be easily created using standard templates, and/or by dragging-and-dropping fields into place to create the tables and forms required.

Already over 400,000 people have adopted Zoho Creator. Customers include DHL, Oxfam and the BBC. Specific applications range from administering a helpdesk, to managing stock levels, recording client satisfaction and making hotel reservations. For those who do not want to build their own database there is even the Zoho Marketplace. This brings together what Zoho claim is 'the most diverse and largest repository of ready-to-use business applications from around the world'. Many freelance database creators now sell their wares through Zoho Marketplace. If you cannot find exactly what you are looking for, you can even search for a developer who will write a Zoho Creator database for you.

Zoho Creator has a free plan that allows one or two users to create up to three databases. After that, user-based fees for creating unlimited databases start at $15 a month for three users with a maximum of 6,000 database records, up to $175 a month for up to fifty users with a mighty 100,000 records. As with any cloud application, the beauty is that users can scale their requirements up and down as their needs dictate and only pay for the exact capacity that they require.

Zoho also offers a range of cloud applications dedicated to specific business tasks. These include the customer relationship management application Zoho CRM to assist with a company's sales and marketing, Zoho Projects for collaborative project management, Zoho Recruit for tracking job applications, and Zoho People for maintaining personnel records. There is also the very handy online invoicing and billing system Zoho Invoice. This includes the facility to e-mail invoices with an embedded PayPal link for collecting payment online.

Most of Zoho's business SaaS is free for a small number of users or projects. Modest costs are then incurred on a user or other volume basis. There is also a great deal of online help available. It is therefore hardly surprising that so many people rave about Zoho as one of the best-kept secrets in the cloud. For example, *Business Week* have praised Zoho for its 'cheaper and more accessible' business applications, while the *New York Times* have described the company as 'thriving amid the giants'. To learn more just visit zoho.com.

Salesforce

Salesforce has been providing business SaaS for over a decade. With nearly 70,000 companies now using its cloud services, it is therefore an SaaS provider to be taken very seriously indeed.

Salesforce describes itself as 'the enterprise cloud-computing company' and is primarily known for two things. These are Salesforce CRM Sales and its Service Cloud. Salesforce CRM Sales is a very popular sales management application as described below. The Service Cloud is a so-termed 'platform as a service' (PaaS) product that will be covered in the next chapter.

Available from salesforce.com, Salesforce CRM Sales is used by companies to manage their sales data and processes online. The idea is that by using this SaaS application, sales representatives can spend more time closing deals and less on administration. This is because they will have all of their contacts and customer records available from the cloud when out on the road. They will also never forget who requires a follow-up call.

As with all SaaS, a collaborative use of the system means that everybody can always see the most up-to-date information. Easy-to-use tools are also available to enable the creation of 'personalized dashboards'. As Salesforce explains, these allow mangers to 'dig deep into their sales data' and obtain a constant overview of the 'real-time status of their business'. There are also tools to assess the results of marketing campaigns and a customer service application for call centres that has already been adopted by 6,800 companies.

Employease

Employease provides human resource (HR) information systems that allow companies to run their payroll, benefits administration and other personnel-related IT in the cloud. The systems provide an online self-service solution for both employees and managers. For example, employees can manage their healthcare and other benefit plans, update their personal information, download any necessary HR-related manuals and forms, and access online training. Managers can then access all necessary employee information including leave, terminations, retirements, promotions, performance reviews and changes in pay.

For HR professionals, Employease provides tools for tracking applications and managing recruitment. Features include the posting of vacancies on internal intranets or external websites, and the 'single click hiring' of applicants once they have accepted a job. In short, the Employease system is intended to allow employees, managers and HR professionals to spend more time actually achieving results.

Employease provides several examples of the benefits of its cloud-based HR solution. Just one is the case of global athletics brand PUMA, which needed to manage its growth efficiently from under 100 to over 1,300 staff. By implementing Employease, PUMA managed to achieve a 50 per cent reduction in the HR time necessary to open a new store. Five local spreadsheets were replaced with a real-time, online HR system used across fifty retail locations. PUMA even recouped the cost of its investment in a matter of weeks. You can learn more at employease.com.

Clarizen

Clarizen describes itself as providing 'online work management software for companies'. This means that it offers an SaaS project-management application that can be collaboratively used to manage anything from one-off projects to resources, timesheets, budgets or expenses. The application displays a linear timeline or 'roadmap' of each project with project progress and projected completion dates.

Clarizen's friendly interface means that most people can learn to use it very quickly. In common with other business SaaS applications, users can create their own personalized dashboard to include specific features and items of information. Project reports can also be created and exported in spreadsheet format for loading into Excel or any of the SaaS office applications already covered in this chapter.

Projects created in Microsoft Project can be imported into Clarizen and exported back if required. There is even a plug-in to allow users to integrate their tasks with Microsoft Outlook (if they are still using non-SaaS e-mail!). Being SaaS, there are also the expected collaboration tools including discussion forums and the ability to share documents. Clarizen is available from clarizen.com where you can sign up for a thirty-day free trail. Subscriptions then start at $29.95 a user per month.

Netsuite

Netsuite is an impressive business SaaS offering that claims to be the 'first and only online business application to support an entire company'. The basis for this bold assertion is that Netsuite offers SaaS tools for customer relationship management (CRM), accounting and enterprise resource planning (ERP), as well as e-commerce and website management. Netsuite's cloud tools indeed allow companies to manage a very wide range of activities including marketing campaigns, customer support, order management, shipping, payroll, purchasing, inventory, website creation and online stores. There can be little doubt that Netsuite is very comprehensive.

Netsuite already has customers across a wide range of industries. In manufacturing it has been used to provide an integrated software solution for inventory, warehouse management, accounting and e-commerce. In service-based businesses, NetSuite SRP (Services Resource Planning) has also been applied to integrate every step of a project lifecycle from marketing and sales to project management, service delivery, billing, revenue management and driving repeat business. Perhaps most significantly, Netsuite offers smaller companies the opportunity to obtain the kind of integrated, real-time software functions previously only available to large corporations. You can find out more at netsuite.com.

WebEx WebOffice

WebEx is a suite of online collaboration tools. The applications allow people to hold virtual meetings by using phone conferencing, shared documents and shared desktops. WebEx is therefore similar to Adobe ConnectNow.

However, tools are also included for creating and managing online databases, which is why the package is included here under business SaaS. To be clear, WebEx WebOffice is not a competitor to Google Docs and most other office SaaS as it does not include a word processor or spreadsheet. However, it does feature some of the most carefully designed online collaboration services available. In addition to custom databases, features also include excellent document management, as well as applications for doing things such as managing projects, filing expense reports and running online polls.

WebOffice custom databases can be created from scratch or based on existing templates. While the intention is to provide everybody on a team with a single, online point of contact for organizing, storing and sharing information, WebOffice's permission and access controls also allow administrators to decide who can see or change certain bits of information.

WebEx WebOffice evolved out of a previous SaaS offering called Intranets.com which was bought by WebEx in 2005. The application therefore has the distinct advantage of being a very mature SaaS product. WebEx WebOffice now has the backing of Internet giant Cisco Systems, which acquired WebEx in 2007. For more information, visit weboffice.com where a thirty-day free trial is available.

Online Storage

A final type of software-related cloud service is online storage. This is sometimes referred to as 'storage as a service' (which inconveniently also has the acronym 'SaaS'), and provides the facility to store, share and back up files on the Internet.

Apart from Pixlr.com, every SaaS application covered in this chapter includes its own online storage. Separate storage as a service options are therefore intended to be used with locally installed software applications. Popular services include Box.net, Livedrive.com and Dropbox.com. As part of Windows Live, Microsoft also offers a cloud storage service called 'Skydrive'. This currently provides private individuals with 25Gb of personal storage for free, and is available from Skydrive.live.com (see also page 208).

Many companies are now using online storage services to share and back up their files. However, storage as a service may well prove to be a short-lived category of cloud offering. This is because, as soon as most applications run online, it will simply not be needed. A broader discussion of online storage options for private individuals is included in chapter nine on the personal cloud.

* * *

The End of Software as We Know It

This chapter has been about software in the cloud. However, the real message is that software is going to disappear. As will be discussed in chapter six, we will still need some kind of hardware, however minimal, to actually access the cloud. We will also continue to work with all kinds of documents, media and other digital data. However, within a decade, most people will rarely consider software. Instead, we will just click on links to viewable and editable documents and other data.

As I explained in chapter one, cloud computing is task-centric. This means that SaaS focuses on what people want to do instead of the tools that are required to achieve those tasks. A carpenter does not go to their workshop to use a saw and screwdriver but to actually make something. Only in computing are we still fixated on the tools. However, cloud computing ought to drive a mentality shift from tool-in-hand to task-at-hand computer application.

The way in which digital data is currently created and manipulated in a software package, locally saved, attached to an e-mail, sent over the Internet, downloaded to a local drive, and then loaded into a matching software application, will soon seem ludicrous. If you only take one message from this chapter then please let it be this. However, I also hope that at least some of the SaaS applications covered in this chapter have already sparked your interest. You may by now even have put this book down once or more to go to a computer to try out an online application or to watch a demo. And if so that is just great!

As an author, my wish would be that you read all of this book. However, if instead you spend some of your time investigating online applications such as Google Docs, Zoho, Acrobat.com, Microsoft Office Web Apps, Pixlr and Jaycut then you will certainly learn a great deal and this book will still have served its purpose.

4

HARDWARE IN THE CLOUD

During the last online revolution in the late 1990s, I worked with a very smart guy called Ian McDonald Wood. Most of our time was spent developing a series of Internet strategy workshops. Constantly coming up with new and relevant ideas was not always easy. However, we managed to specify a number of concepts and models to help our clients understand the bewildering rise of e-business.

Ian and I live some distance apart. We therefore spent a great deal of time on the phone trying to make sense of the madness of Dot Com. Ten years on, I don't recall a great deal of what we talked about. However, I do remember that at the start of many three-hour calls Ian used to suggest wrapping a wet towel around his head to stop his brain hurting too much. And I absolutely knew what he meant.

Ian's wet towel joke has come into my mind several times while planning this chapter. So far in this book I have presented a number of concepts related to cloud computing, as well as information on a fair few SaaS or 'software as a service' online applications. Bringing this material together has not so far been that difficult. However, this is unfortunately not the case when it comes to explaining the supply of hardware from the cloud. In a nutshell, cloud hardware is what cloud software runs on. However, things immediately get tricky because cloud hardware is offered in two variants – known as 'platform as a service' (PaaS) and 'infrastructure as a service' (IaaS) – that can be difficult to distinguish and explain.

Some authors deal with the complexity of cloud hardware by getting very technical or – more commonly – by missing lots of things out. However, for me neither of these approaches appeals! In this chapter I will therefore try to present a comprehensive model of online hardware that does not become technical. I therefore hope you now appreciate why I have been thinking of my old friend Ian McDonald Wood and cooling the brain with a wet towel. I will also try very hard to ensure that your own grey matter has not over-heated too much by the time we arrive at chapter five!

The Three Ways to Cloud Compute

There are essentially three ways in which a business may replace traditional in-house systems with cloud computing. Specifically, the available options are:

- Software as a Service (SaaS)
- Platform as a Service (PaaS) and
- Infrastructure as a Service (IaaS)

All of the above involve a cloud vendor supplying servers on which their customers store data and run applications. However, the differences between SaaS, PaaS and IaaS concern the level of control that a business has over the applications they use, how these applications are created, and the type of hardware on which their applications are run.

Very simply, when businesses opt for SaaS they can only run those applications that their cloud supplier has on offer. When they opt for PaaS they can create their own applications but only in a manner determined by their cloud supplier. And when they opt for IaaS they can run any applications they please on cloud hardware of their own choice. OK, that may at this stage still be as clear as well-stirred mud! So I will now work through it again in more detail.

From Cloud Software to Cloud Hardware

As explained in the last chapter, the software as a service or 'SaaS' approach to cloud computing involves making use of existing, off-the-shelf web applications. This is by far the easiest way to cloud compute, and is an excellent option when all that is required is a standard package such as a word processor. However, the SaaS approach to cloud computing is likely to be inadequate where off-the-shelf applications will not suffice.

It is because SaaS is basically a take-it-or-leave-it option that businesses and sometimes individuals may want direct access to cloud computing hardware on which they can run their own applications. The two ways they can achieve this are by opting to cloud compute at either the platform or infrastructure level. This involves using either platform as a service (PaaS) or infrastructure as a service (IaaS). To explain what this means, I first need to tell you what the terms 'platform' and 'infrastructure' are all about.

In computing, platforms are software environments used to develop and run end-user applications. Infrastructure is then the physical hardware on which platforms and applications actually operate. To provide a traditional computing example, Microsoft Word is an application that runs on the Microsoft Windows platform. The Windows platform in turn then operates on the infrastructure of a desktop PC or laptop computer. Figure 4.1 provides a simple illustration of the layered relationship between computing infrastructure, platforms and applications.

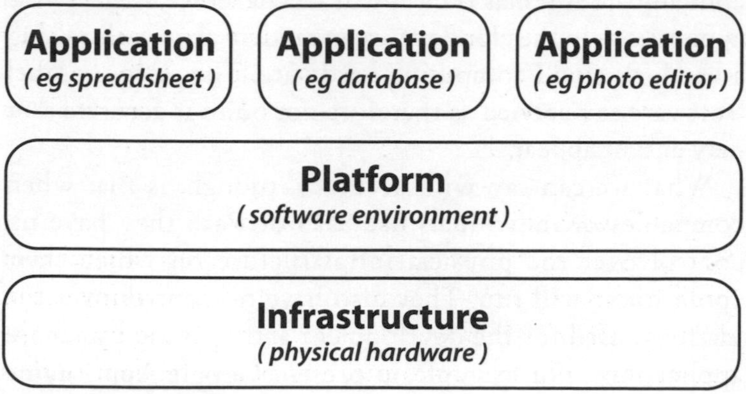

Figure 4.1: Computing infrastructure, platforms and applications

When companies or individuals choose to cloud compute at the platform level, they opt for platform as a service (PaaS). This enables them to access online hardware, coupled with a software environment in which they can develop and run their own SaaS applications. To take one example, which will later be explored in more depth, Google offers a PaaS service called App Engine. This allows anybody to write new cloud applications and to deliver them over the web using Google's infrastructure.

Both SaaS and PaaS inevitably involve the storing of data and the running of applications on a cloud vendor's hardware. For example, when word processing in Google Docs users are actually running program code on a Google server on which their documents are also stored. Similarly, if a developer creates and runs their own custom SaaS application using Google App Engine, then their program code once again ends up running on a Google server. In some respects this is a interesting point to contemplate as it makes clear that whenever we use software applications in the cloud we are in tandem always also using a vendor's cloud computing hardware. The category label 'software as a service' is therefore not quite as accurate as it may at first appear.

What we can say with accuracy, though, is that when companies or individuals use SaaS or PaaS they have no control over the physical infrastructure on which their applications will run. They also have no control over the platform used for the development and operation of those applications. For example, at present Google App Engine applications have to be written in just one of two programming languages called Java and Python. Programmers who opt to use Google App Engine therefore make a take-it-or-leave-it decision to forgo programming in any other language.

For many individuals and some organizations, having no control over the platform or infrastructure they are using is not really a problem. However, for others – including those who want to run their existing software applications in the cloud or who have particular security concerns – it is simply not good enough. For this reason a significant proportion of cloud computing is based around the infrastructure as a service or IaaS model. This is where a vendor provides their customers with access to hardware in the cloud on which they can store their data and run any applications they choose.

In practical terms, using infrastructure as a service allows individuals or organizations to benefit from the advantages of cloud computing without having to alter their computing activities. All that changes is that their applications run 'out there' in the cloud rather than on servers located in their own offices or data centres.

Understanding the Fundamentals

So far in this chapter I have attempted to explain the conceptual differences between cloud software (in the form of SaaS) and cloud hardware (in the form of PaaS and IaaS). Understanding the nature of SaaS, PaaS and IaaS is also of fundamental importance for anybody really wanting to get to grips with the rising potential of the cloud. SaaS, PaaS and IaaS are quite simply the fundamental building blocks of the Cloud Computing Revolution. It is therefore pretty important for you to know what they are all about. Figure 4.2 provides an illustrative overview of SaaS, PaaS and IaaS.

I hope the last chapter gave you a solid and practical understanding of SaaS. Again using real product examples as appropriate, the rest of this chapter is intended to do the same for PaaS and IaaS. Unfortunately, even though a few PaaS and IaaS offerings are free for some initial use, unless you have some technical skill you will not be able to go and play with them online in the same way that you could with Google Docs, Zoho, Acrobat.com, Pixlr and their other SaaS friends. However, what I do hope you will readily appreciate is the enormous potential of PaaS and IaaS to decrease the cost and to increase the flexibility of many areas of computing and business. PaaS and IaaS will mainly be purchased by companies. However, their adoption in business will affect us all.

Platform as a Service (PaaS)

PaaS vendors provide everything necessary to rapidly create, test and deliver new online applications. Such applications may be made available privately – for example to the workforce of just one organization – or publicly on a free or for-a-fee basis. This means that there are a great many potential uses for PaaS. These range from the creation of new business systems for the use of just one particular organization, through to the development of new online customer interfaces, and to the use of PaaS tools to help bring new SaaS applications to market. So, if you have a great idea for a new online application, you can use PaaS to rapidly turn it into a reality.

Some technical programming knowledge is required to use most PaaS offerings. However, once this knowledge is acquired pretty much anybody – be they a computer science student working in their bedroom or a large corporation – can now create new web-based applications and deliver them to the rest of the planet rapidly at minimal cost. Like so many other cloud computing developments, PaaS is therefore already starting to level playing fields.

Having said that the development of new applications using PaaS requires technical programming skill, PaaS does speed up the process by automating some coding tasks. All current PaaS offerings require programmers to work in their own specified programming languages and to use only the supplied tools to create new applications. While this can be restrictive, it again speeds up the development process because the PaaS vendor can guarantee that the languages and tools they provide will work properly on their cloud infrastructure. In a sense, PaaS may be thought of as providing programmers with a box of cloud computing Lego. New applications can only be constructed from the specific plastic bricks on offer. However, because the PaaS vendor supplies all of the bricks, it can guarantee that they will always assemble easily and hold together.

Before PaaS existed, programmers had to create new web applications using an internal test system. When they got their program working, they then had to move or 'migrate' it to the live web server that would make it available on the Internet. This may sound easy in theory, but the process of migrating new applications from test systems to live servers

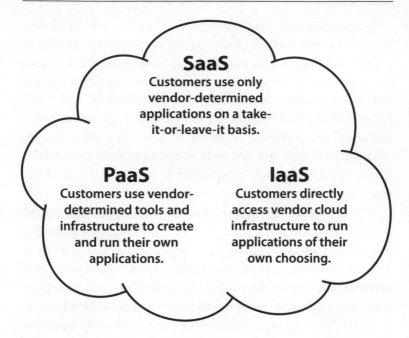

Figure 4.2: The building blocks of cloud computing

can be problematic. Frequently, new applications that work on the computer under a programmer's desk do not function as intended on the company's web server without considerable tweaking and bug fixing. This is why so many programmers look so bleary-eyed and drink way too much coffee.

One of the major advantages of many PaaS offerings is that new applications do not have to be migrated between systems. This is because applications are created from scratch on the same platform from which they will be delivered to their final users. It is therefore exceedingly unlikely that a new application that has been properly tested will not work perfectly the moment it goes live on the web.

Delivering new applications that 'just work' is clearly good for everybody. Equally useful is the related ability to create and test new application features behind the scenes that can then be turned on with little or no risk that they will break everything else. Before cloud computing and PaaS, rapidly and flexibly turning on new live program functionality for millions of users at the click of a mouse was unthinkable. Yet today it is becoming commonplace. Once again we notch up another key advantage of cloud computing.

The above all noted, like anything else in life and on the Internet, PaaS is not a panacea. One of the biggest potential drawbacks of developing new applications using PaaS is vendor lock-in. There are currently a relatively small number of PaaS vendors available, and all of them have their own standards and programming tools. Anybody who uses PaaS to develop applications therefore inevitably becomes reliant on their chosen vendor. This makes the choice of vendor critical, and is likely to drive most users to the doors of large organizations like Google and Microsoft.

Those opting to develop applications using PaaS have to be particularly mindful of the 'flexibility verses power trade-off'. In other words, they have to weigh the benefits of being able to rapidly create new applications against the potential limitations of their chosen vendor's specific development languages and tools. To analogize, if there is a possibility that they may in future want to build toys out of wooden blocks, opting for a vendor who only allows them to build out of Lego would be a bad idea.

If only for the above reasons, it is perhaps not surprising that certain key vendors already dominate the PaaS marketplace and are likely to continue to do so. We will therefore now take a brief look at what they have on offer.

Google App Engine

Google is not sponsoring this book, honest! The company has just invested very heavily in the cloud. When it comes to PaaS, Google specifically offers a popular product called App Engine. Available from appengine.google.com, this allows anybody to develop, run and maintain web applications on Google's infrastructure.

Google App Engine places more technical constraints on application developers than most of its competitors. However, it does this with no apology as this approach enables reliability to be maintained. The technical constraints that App Engine places on developers also allow applications to run at high speed and to be very rapidly scaled up for delivery to a great many users simultaneously. During his election campaign, President Obama famously used an application created in Google App Engine called Moderator to run virtual town hall meetings. In some of these meetings the system handled 700 hits per second, logged over 100,000 questions and recorded over 200,000 votes. As this example demonstrates, Google App Engine is an excellent PaaS offering for anybody wanting to create web applications for mass public use.

As Google very clearly explains, 'App Engine costs nothing to get started. All applications can use up to 500Mb of storage and enough processor power and bandwidth to support an efficient application serving around five million page views a month, absolutely free.' Beyond the free limits, as with all cloud computing, customers only pay for the resources they actually use. This means that, with absolutely no infra-structure investment, an application developer can confidently provide online applications that will work regardless of the number of users. Given that many Dot Com start-ups were effectively killed off by their initial investment in servers and other web infrastructure, this is very significant indeed.

Using its online App Gallery, people who develop applications using Google App Engine can showcase and sell them on the web. Anybody wanting to develop applications can also download the App Engine software developer kit (SDK) for free. Furthermore, Google provides a great many other useful support resources.

While App Engine may be somewhat restrictive for developers, the attraction of hosting web applications in Google's data centres is clear. It used to be said that nobody ever got fired for buying computers from IBM. Similarly today, choosing Google as your PaaS vendor is likely to be accepted as a pretty safe bet.

Force.com

Force.com is a PaaS offering from the well-established business SaaS provider Salesforce.com. It allows anybody to build and run applications on the same infrastructure used for Salesforce's off-the-shelf SaaS applications as covered in the last chapter. As the sales pitch puts it:

> Just log in, build your app, and share it with the world. The simplified programming model and cloud-based environment mean you can build and run applications five times faster, at about half the cost of traditional software platforms.

The above may clearly sound attractive. Recently, Force.com has even decided to allow anybody to build and run their first application for free for up to 100 users. Competition between PaaS vendors is hotting up.

Force.com is marketed on the back of the company's successful Salesforce.com SaaS offering. As it argues, the cloud infrastructure has been fine-tuned for over ten years and supports around 70,000 businesses running more than 135,000 applications used by over one and a half million users every day. Within a feature called AppExchange there is also a library of around 800 applications that can be purchased and used by developers as the basis for other applications. For existing Salesforce.com users in particular, Force.com is therefore a PaaS offering well worth considering.

Microsoft Windows Azure

In March 2010 Microsoft CEO Steve Ballmer claimed that he is 'betting the company' on cloud computing. As noted in the last chapter, on the applications frontier Microsoft's strategy is very much to cautiously incorporate a cloud component into its traditional desktop software. However, when it comes to platform as a service, in January 2010 the company more than dipped its corporate toes into the water when it launched a long-awaited cloud platform called Azure.

Windows Azure is a complex offering with several components that can be used separately or in combination. However, in essence Azure is Microsoft's platform for running Windows applications and storing data in the cloud. Windows Azure itself is a so-termed 'cloud operating system' that runs on server computers located in Microsoft data centres. Customers then use the Windows Azure Platform this creates to develop and run their online applications on Microsoft's infrastructure.

As with other PaaS offerings, the applications created using the Windows Azure Platform may be internal or external to a business, and either private or public. For example, commercial software developers may create new SaaS applications using Azure (and indeed Microsoft has said that it will build its own SaaS applications using Azure). Alternatively, an IT department may use the Windows Azure Platform to build and run online applications just for use internally by their own employees.

Windows Azure is split into three main parts called Compute, Storage and Fabric. As may be expected, the first two of these are used to run applications and to store data. The Fabric component then provides a means of managing and monitoring the cloud applications that a customer has running on Microsoft's infrastructure.

Like Google App Engine, Windows Azure is designed to allow the applications created with it to easily scale up for use by a great many people at the same time. This may be critical for some users. However, others may be more concerned with simply storing large quantities of data online. In this second instance they may therefore just use Azure Storage to enable them to manage large volumes of data in the cloud.

The advantage of Windows Azure is that it allows programmers already familiar with creating Windows applications to build cloud applications in a familiar development environment. The disadvantage is that Azure is later to market than its competitors and still a somewhat unknown quantity. More information can be found at microsoft.com/windowsazure.

Zoho Creator

The line between SaaS and PaaS vendor offerings can sometimes get a little blurry. For example, the popular online database application Zoho Creator covered in the last chapter can also be categorized as PaaS. This is because Zoho Creator offers tools that allow its users to create custom database applications that run on Zoho's infrastructure. Some therefore choose to classify Zoho Creator as SaaS (a database is, after all, a generic office application), while others list it as PaaS.

However it is classified, Zoho Creator is an excellent cloud computing service already in use by over 400,000 people. It is mentioned again in this chapter purely for completeness. For more information look back to page 67 or visit creator.zoho.com.

PaaS website building tools

Any cloud service that provides tools for building something on somebody else's infrastructure can technically be listed as PaaS. This means that online website builders fall into the PaaS category and rightfully deserve a mention here.

Many companies now offer the facility to build quite a professional and complex website using online graphical tools. Notable examples include Google Sites (sites.google.com), Moonfruit (moonfruit.com) and Webs.com (webs.com). Once you have registered on them (for free), you will be presented with a range of tools and hundreds of template options that quickly allow anybody to create a very impressive website. Fees become payable if users want a lot of pages, no advertising, or need a great deal of storage space. If you or your company do not have a website or want a better one, then Google Sites, Moonfruit or Webs.com are all well worth a look.

Other PaaS providers

This section has covered those big-name PaaS providers that you are likely to come across in any broader research into cloud computing. There are, however, other companies already offering PaaS or floating in the wings. For a start, industry veteran IBM has launched a product range called Smart Business Cloud Solutions. Meanwhile software giant Oracle has created its Oracle Platform for SaaS. This said, in comparison to those products already discussed, both of these cloud services are complex and somewhat difficult to neatly categorize.

As implied at the start of this chapter, hardware in the cloud really has not settled yet. Partially this is because different companies call similar services different things. It is also because some companies, including Oracle and IBM, are forming cloud computing partnerships to offer their software and development tools from their competitors' cloud infrastructure. For example, many companies are now partnering with Amazon Web Services, as detailed in the next section. Given the inherent flexibility of cloud computing technology, we should expect to see a great many more online partnerships in the near future.

Infrastructure as a Service (IaaS)

Platform as a service is a very significant cloud computing development. However, infrastructure as a service (IaaS) is where the really big cloud computing business is currently at. IaaS is where a vendor offers computer hardware in the cloud on which their customers can store data and develop and run whatever applications they please. IaaS therefore allows companies to move their existing programs and data into the cloud and to close down their own local servers and data centres.

So far I have used the word 'infrastructure' as a pretty loose term for computer hardware. This has also not been unreasonable, as simply thinking of 'infrastructure' as those hardware boxes that reside in a data centre has been good enough. Cloud infrastructure is basically what cloud software applications run on and where data in the cloud is stored. However, in order to explain infrastructure as a service and its different categories, I now need to tell you a little more about infrastructure than this.

The fundamental building block of computing infra-structure is the server. Some servers are designed largely to process data and others largely to store it. However, for our purposes, we can define a server as a piece of hardware that offers remote processing power and/or storage capacity. Servers that can be accessed over the Internet are therefore what infrastructure as a service (IaaS) vendors supply to their customers.

Along with servers, IaaS vendors also need to provide other physical hardware and related management and support. For a start, servers need a constant and reliable power supply. All data centres – in the cloud or otherwise – therefore need sophisticated and costly uninterruptable power supply systems that can keep their servers running even if the mains supply fails.

Servers also need a great deal of cooling, which again comes at considerable cost. Servers additionally need to be located in a secure environment with appropriate measures taken to protect them from fire, flood and other natural disasters. To guard against possible damage or failure, servers also need to be backed up to other servers. In any data centre there also need to be IT specialists available 24/7 to ensure that the servers keep working properly and to effect repairs if necessary.

In addition to all of the above, cloud computing servers have to be connected to the Internet with a robust, high-speed connection. They then have to have their web traffic managed – or what is technically termed 'load balanced' – so that all users receive a consistent level of service. Once again this requires special hardware and costs money. What I hope this all indicates is that being an IaaS vendor involves a great deal of ongoing cost and complexity. Of course, this cost and complexity is what users of IaaS services turn into somebody else's problem by opting to purchase their infrastructure from the cloud.

IaaS categories and virtualization

As I have said, the fundamental building block of cloud computing infrastructure is the server. Not that long ago every server computer was a physically discrete hardware box. However, this is no longer the case. Today, most servers in medium- or large-scale data centres have been amalgamated into 'racks' populated with server 'blades'.

A rack is an equipment stand, usually 48cm wide, on which a number of server computers can be housed. Until a few years ago, most servers in traditional racks were individual hardware boxes each with its own power supply and network connection. However, these days the racks in most large data centres contain blade servers. These are server computers stripped down to the bare minimum so that they can only function when slotted into a blade rack. Basically a blade server is a computer circuit board with a processor, memory and a hard drive or two attached.

The advantage of blade servers is that they save a great deal of space and use less energy. This is because each server blade does not need its own, individual power supply. Modern racks can accommodate up to 128 server blades. Today's largest cloud data centres now also have many thousands of such racks.

While IaaS vendors basically rent servers on which their customers store data and run applications, a great many of the servers they supply are virtual rather than real. What this means is that while cloud data centres contain rack upon rack of server blades, these physical servers are subdivided by a software process called 'virtualization'.

After the Internet itself, virtualization is the most fundamental technology that allows cloud computing to occur. Using virtualization, any physical server can be split into any number of virtual servers, each of which can then be used entirely independently by a different user.

Virtualization is a technology that is familiar to many Mac users who use it to run a virtual Windows PC on their Apple computer.

In cloud computing, virtual servers are usually referred to as 'instances'. What all this means is that there are in fact two basic offerings that IaaS vendors can rent to their customers. The first of these are dedicated physical servers, or in other words actual computer circuit boards with their own processor and hard disks that live in a rack somewhere. The second are then virtual server instances, or in other words parts of physical servers that function as if they were real servers, but which in reality are just a software-controlled slice of a real server computer.

While dedicated physical servers and virtual server instances can perform exactly the same functions, they do have some differing characteristics. Most obviously, virtual server instances are cheaper to supply as each does not require its own piece of physical hardware. On the other hand, virtual server instances are sometimes seen as less secure by those who do not want to share server hardware with other customers. For this reason, and as illustrated in figure 4.3, the following four categories of IaaS are currently available:

- Private cloud
- Dedicated hosting
- Hybrid hosting, and
- Cloud hosting

In each of the four parts of figure 4.3 there is a large rectangle representing a cloud data centre. This contains a number of dedicated physical servers (shown as small rectangles) and a number of virtual server instances (shown as circles within a cloud). In practice, these virtual server instances are part of a physical server and look no different to the dedicated servers. However, representing them like that would not help us here! Dedicated physical servers or virtual server instances in the figure are shown in solid, rather than outline, when they are part of a particular IaaS category.

Private cloud

Illustrated at the top of figure 4.3, the most risk-averse and potentially the most secure form of IaaS is called the private cloud. Sometimes more fully referred to as a 'vendor-managed private cloud', this is effectively the rental of part of a cloud data centre. A specific number of dedicated physical servers all located in the same part of a data centre are provided to a customer. This means that their cloud hardware is as separated as possible from that of other users.

Private cloud IaaS customers could actually go and visit their servers if they wished and even take them cakes on their birthday. Well OK, in practice the IaaS vendor would probably not permit foodstuffs in their server space. However, I hope this makes it clear why private clouds are viewed by many as the safest form of cloud computing. The option may be costly and diminish some of the potential cloud benefits (such as the most optimal use of computing resources). However, companies who opt for an IaaS private cloud still gain the advantage of having their servers housed in a vendor's large data centre, with power, cooling, security and management overheads shared with other customers.

Dedicated hosting

Second down in figure 4.3 there is the IaaS category of dedicated hosting. This is where a customer rents a number of dedicated physical servers within a cloud data centre. This again means that the customer does not have to share their

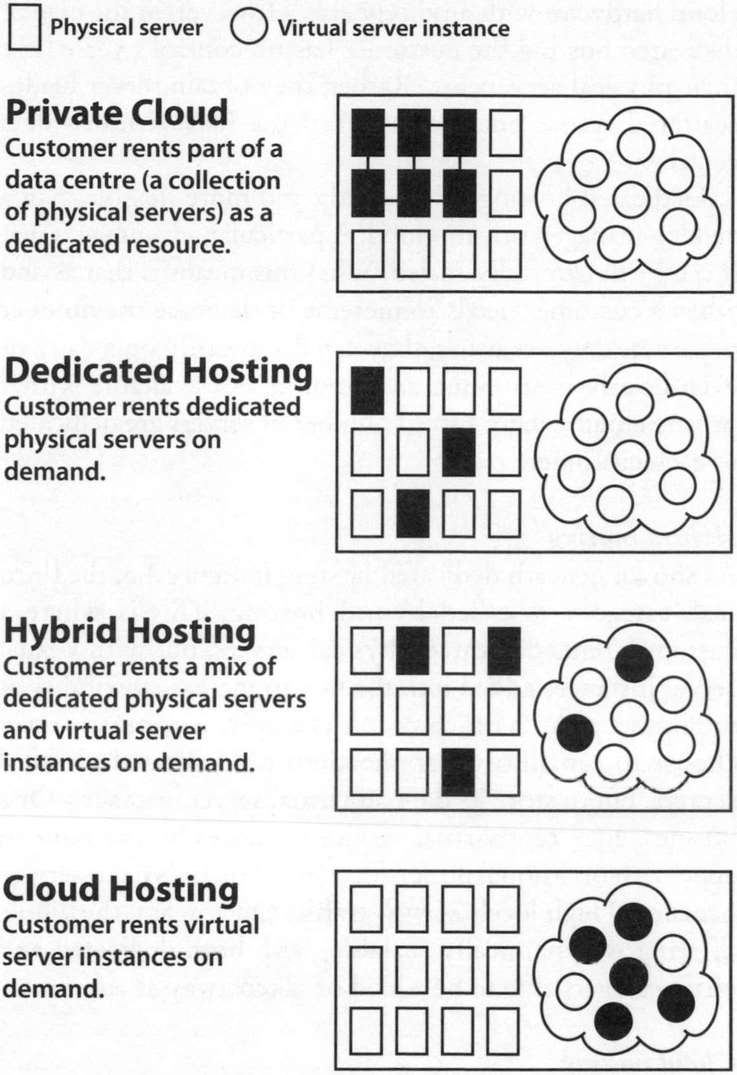

☐ Physical server   ◯ Virtual server instance

Private Cloud
Customer rents part of a data centre (a collection of physical servers) as a dedicated resource.

Dedicated Hosting
Customer rents dedicated physical servers on demand.

Hybrid Hosting
Customer rents a mix of dedicated physical servers and virtual server instances on demand.

Cloud Hosting
Customer rents virtual server instances on demand.

Figure 4.3: The four categories of IaaS

cloud hardware with anybody else. However, in the case of dedicated hosting the customer has no control over where their physical servers are. Rather, they obtain server blades scattered across one (or more) of the IaaS vendor's data centres.

Dedicated hosting is less costly and more flexible than a vendor-managed private cloud. A particular advantage is that it can be dynamically scaled. What this means is that as and when a customer needs to increase or decrease the number of servers they are using, they can do so easily on a daily or even hourly basis. Such an option is not available with a private cloud, where a fixed number of servers are dedicated to each customer.

Hybrid hosting

As shown beneath dedicated hosting in figure 4.3, the third IaaS category is called hybrid hosting. This is where a customer rents dedicated physical servers, but with virtual server instances added into the mix to increase flexibility at minimum cost. As a common example, a company may choose to run all of its applications on dedicated physical servers, but to store its data on virtual server instances. Or a business may rent virtual service instances by the hour to cope with occasional peak processing demands or to service occasional high levels of web traffic. Once again, the whole offering is dynamically scalable, with both dedicated and virtual servers able to be added or taken away at any time.

Cloud hosting

Finally at the bottom of figure 4.3 we have cloud hosting. This is where a customer purchases as many or as few virtual server instances as they require on demand, and usually on an hourly basis. This means that the customer has no control whatsoever over the exact server hardware on which their data is stored and their applications run. Rather, they simply share server blades with other customers. Some companies see this as too risky. However, cloud hosting is without doubt the most technically and environmentally efficient form of cloud computing. This is because it allows the IaaS vendor to run all of their physical servers in use to capacity and to close down those not required. In turn this means that cloud hosting is the cheapest option for the customer and increasingly popular.

IaaS Vendors

Several companies are now operating in the IaaS market-place. Most specialize in one or a few of the IaaS categories illustrated in figure 4.3. As previously in this book, I am not going to detail all vendors and their cloud services here. Rather, I am going to describe a few key IaaS offerings – and one in particular – to illustrate how IaaS cloud computing is developing in practice.

Amazon Web Services

Founded in 1994, Amazon – the online retailer always described by founder Jeff Bezos as a 'logistics business' – is without doubt the largest IaaS provider in the world. From its acres of cloud data centres, the company offers a range of cloud infrastructure services under the banner 'Amazon Web Services' or 'AWS'. All of these currently fall under the cloud hosting category. In other words, Amazon's IaaS is fully virtualized, with the company selling virtual server instances.

At the heart of AWS is Amazon Elastic Compute Cloud or 'EC2'. This is an almost 'classic' cloud offering that makes it easy to run applications in Amazon's data centres. EC2 is described by Amazon as 'elastic' because customers can increase or decrease the infrastructure capacity they are using within minutes.

If you are not interested in computer specifications, then skip this paragraph. But if you are, you may be interested to learn that EC2's virtual server instances are offered in seven different specifications. The most basic is the default or 'small instance', which has one virtual processor core, 1.7Gb of memory and 160Gb of local instance storage. This costs from $0.085 an hour. The highest specification instance currently available has eight virtual processor cores, 7Gb of memory and 1690Gb of local instance storage, and costs from $0.68 an hour.

While all EC2 servers are virtualized, users do have the choice of purchasing them from Amazon's North Virginia, North California or European Union (Irish) data centres. This can be significant for some users who need to keep their data within certain geographic regions on the grounds of particular data protection legislation.

EC2 users can purchase and activate one, hundreds or even thousands of virtual server instances simultaneously. They do this by setting up Amazon Machine Images, or AMIs, that contain all of the applications, data and configuration settings that their virtual servers will need. AMIs can be created from scratch or chosen from a range of pre-configured templates. As mentioned in the PaaS section, Amazon now has partnerships with companies including IBM. The latter provides AMIs that allow customers to run existing applications, already licensed from IBM, on virtual EC2 servers.

As this all suggests, EC2 is a highly significant cloud computing product that, in some respects, is light years away from Google Docs and the other office SaaS covered in the last chapter (and which are still amazing). Using EC2, companies big and small now have an incredible potential to migrate all of their data centre activities to the cloud. Most fixed computing overheads subsequently disappear to be replaced with flexible, variable costs paid on an hourly basis. There may be security and reliability concerns, as will be discussed in the next chapter. However, IaaS offerings like EC2 are something few companies ought to ignore.

Another major component of AWS is the Amazon Simple Storage Service or S3. This is a 'storage as a service' offering that allows customers to keep their data in online 'buckets'. As Amazon explain:

> Amazon S3 provides a simple web interface that can be used to store and retrieve any amount of data, at any time, from anywhere on the web. It gives any developer access to the same highly scalable, reliable, fast, inexpensive data storage infrastructure that Amazon uses to run its own global network of web sites.

It currently costs \$0.10 to upload 1Gb of data to Amazon S3, and \$0.15 a month to store it there, although prices fall if customers store more than 50 terabytes (50,000Gb!). Anybody can use Amazon S3 for both long- or short-term data storage and back-up. However, S3 is primarily a business service. For individuals, there are more effective storage as a service options. These will be discussed as part of the 'personal cloud' in chapter nine. However, some of these, such as CloudBerry from CloudBerryLab.com, simply provide an easy-to-use consumer web interface to Amazon S3. How kind.

Other components of Amazon Web Services include Amazon SimpleDB to provide online database functionality, and Amazon Mechanical Turk for accessing 'thousands of high quality, low cost, global, on-demand workers' from the cloud. The latter clearly takes IaaS into a whole new and potentially very scary direction! Entire books have already been written about using Amazon Web Services (such as the excellent, if technical, *Cloud Application Architectures* by George Reece). You can find out more at aws.amazon.com.

GoGrid

IaaS vendor GoGrid offers cloud hosting, hybrid hosting and dedicated hosting solutions. The company claims to offer the most control of all current IaaS vendors, and its services are indeed generally regarded as being the easiest to get to grips with.

GoGrid's website at gogrid.com features some particularly useful tables that make direct comparisons with other IaaS offerings. You will not be surprised to learn that the breadth of GoGrid's offering does very well indeed. Marketing aside, the fact that GoGrid offers several IaaS options means that it is a potentially safe IaaS provider. This is because customers have the flexibility of hosting different aspects of their business on different types of real or virtual server as their needs dictate.

Rackspace

Rackspace is a well-known provider of traditional hosting services and has responded very effectively to the cloud computing revolution. Like GoGrid, Rackspace now offers a choice of IaaS solutions. These range from managed services for providing dedicated hosting and private clouds, to a range of virtualized cloud hosting services similar to Amazon's IaaS provision. The latter include Rackspace Cloud Servers as a direct competitor to Amazon EC2, as well as Rackspace Cloud Files as an alternative to Amazon S3.

Rackspace has a great website that explains all of the options available and indeed is a good cloud computing learning tool in its own right. You can find it online at rackspace.com.

The Implications for All of Us

Platform and infrastructure as a service may at first appear pretty irrelevant for most people. However, this is absolutely not the case. Even if you never directly and consciously use a PaaS or IaaS offering, you are still very likely to indirectly make use of one. This is due to the increasing number of companies and software developers who create and run their websites and SaaS offerings on third-party platforms and infrastructure. Any user of Twitter, for example, is indirectly accessing Amazon Web Services, as Twitter uses Amazon's S3 for storing profile and background images, as well as for making back-ups.

The use of hardware in the cloud is also of more general significance for three reasons. Firstly, PaaS and IaaS are already allowing companies to develop software more rapidly and at lower cost, and it is hoped we will all benefit from that. Secondly, we will all also benefit from the environmental savings that result when companies move their hardware into the cloud. Computer data centres are never likely to be highly environmentally friendly. However, energy consumption and carbon emissions can be significantly reduced by running relatively few large cloud data centres rather than tens of thousands of individual company data centres that are rarely used to capacity. In fact, as environmental legislation tightens, it may well be the green agenda that forces many companies to start using hardware in the cloud.

The third and final reason that PaaS and IaaS are important is that, as more and more processing takes place online, so fewer and fewer of us will need a really powerful personal computer. The most visible implication of hardware in the cloud will therefore be that our screens, keyboards and CPU boxes will become just screens and keyboards. In other words, there will usually be no requirement for a third box to house a powerful processor and hard drive. Granted, we will all continue to use more and more extensive computer processing power, but such processing capacity will be out in the cloud.

* * *

Blurring Towards Maturity?

Web 2.0 pioneer Tim O'Reilly recently described the Internet as a new-born baby. However, if the Internet is a new-born baby, then hardware in the cloud is an embryo. It exists, definitely. However, it has yet to really mature. Because of this many people are likely to continue to struggle to get to grips with hardware in the cloud for some time to come. It is also likely to take a while before we get any absolutely rock-solid terminology and categorizations.

A few years ago, when the term 'cloud computing' was just starting to enter the mainstream, most developments were categorized as either 'software as a service' (SaaS) or 'hardware as a service' (HaaS). Even though this chapter is called 'Hardware in the Cloud', I have avoided using the HaaS term. This is because industry analysts and IT vendors now more regularly draw a distinction between 'platform as a service' (PaaS) and 'infrastructure as a service' (IaaS), as I have explained in this chapter. To initially throw yet another term into the mix would therefore, I think, have been less than helpful.

It is also worth noting that, given the speed of cloud computing development, it may well be that the lines between PaaS and IaaS will begin to blur. This may be due to a trend for IaaS vendors to offer development tools, as well as for PaaS vendors to allow their customers to work with an increasingly wider range of tools and languages. If such a trend does take hold, then people may once again start talking about hardware as a service or HaaS, rather than its current sub-categories of PaaS and IaaS. Then again, they may not!

Cloud computing is likely to remain awash with acronyms like SaaS, PaaS, IaaS and HaaS. However, aside from possibly allowing you to appear knowledgeable at a dinner party, none of the actual terms really matters that much. Regardless of how cloud computing developments may be labelled and classified, far more important are what the growing range of cloud computing services actually allow us to achieve. Also important are the broader implications of cloud computing for individuals, businesses, the software industry and the future of computing. With Part I of this book having now detailed all of the practical cloud computing basics, it is therefore time for us to venture into the chapters of Part II and to address cloud computing's wider impact.

Part II

CLOUD COMPUTING IMPLICATIONS

5

SECURITY, PRIVACY AND RELIABILITY

So far I have painted a fairly rosy picture of cloud computing and its benefits. There are, however, many who raise concerns at even the suggestion of processing and storing data online. In this first chapter to focus on the implications of cloud computing, I am therefore going to consider the potential risks associated with the use of remote, third-party computing resources.

At the end of 2009, International Data Corporation surveyed 263 IT and business executives to find out what most worried them about cloud computing. Not surprisingly, the risk of unauthorized access to cloud data and applications came top of the list. Second were concerns concerning the reliability of both cloud computing vendors and the Internet connection used to access them. Such concerns have also been mirrored in other business surveys. A great many private individuals also harbour fears that personal information uploaded to the cloud may be open to abuse.

By definition, all cloud computing relies on a connection to the Internet. If that connection is compromised by hackers, exposed to the world or simply fails, then the security or availability of the cloud service being accessed will also be compromised. Just as seriously, if the username and password of a cloud computing user are stolen – or if the security of the computing device they are using is otherwise compromised – then again problems may arise. In addition, if a cloud vendor's infrastructure is not well protected or unreliable – or indeed if the vendor behaves in an unscrupulous manner – then again there will be cause for concern. It is therefore hardly surprising that cloud computing is often perceived as somewhat risky.

Nobody can ever tell you that cloud computing is entirely safe. However, neither is breathing, crossing the street, or storing all of your data on a stand-alone computer. Our choice of whether or not to cloud compute therefore needs to be taken not on the basis of whether it carries any level of risk at all, but after considering whether the risks involved are worth the potential payback.

The benefits of cloud computing have already been outlined in Part I. In brief they include lower costs, opportunities for collaboration, any-device access, zero fixed costs, greater flexibility, environmental savings and the ability to run next-generation applications. This is a pretty powerful set of benefits for both individuals and businesses. Quite whether such benefits are enough to balance out all the potential risks has to remain a matter of private or company choice. However, I would suggest that for most of us the risk/reward balance is already tipping in favour of cloud computing.

The Continual Security Trade-Off

The only reason that any form of data is put on to a computer is to make it easier to store, process, retrieve and communicate. Any form of computing that does not pose potential security risks is therefore not worth having in the first place. Across history, almost all new computing developments have been intended to make it easier to access and work with information. As a result, almost all new computing developments have raised security concerns. Pretty much every computing advancement has therefore required us to balance an ease-of-use versus security trade-off.

When personal computing first released information and processing power from the shackles of the data centre in the 1980s, security concerns were immediately high on the agenda. When laptops subsequently allowed information and processing power to venture beyond the office, security concerns were then raised further still. With personal computing also came floppy disks, CDs, USB keys and all of the other removable media that allow data to be quite easily lost and stolen.

Following the PC revolution came the next security nightmare of the first-generation Internet. For years we were reliably informed that nobody would ever risk entering personal data into a website, let alone a credit card number. However, today most of us routinely enter all kinds of data online without even breaking into a sweat. Is some of this data very occasionally stolen? Yes. But on balance most people consider the benefits of shopping, communicating and managing their affairs online to be worth the risk.

What I am saying here is that it would be staggering if the current cloud computing revolution were not perceived as risky. This does not mean that we ought to ignore legitimate security worries. However, there is a danger that many people will hide behind security fears while cloud computing's pioneers and then early-to-mid adopters reap the benefits and streak past them in the fast lane. Nothing in life is safe. However, with the right precautions, most things – including cloud computing – can be undertaken with an acceptable level of risk.

Dealing with Security Concerns

Cloud computing security is a topic that can be addressed on two levels. One of these is deeply technical and concerns the application of appropriate technologies, techniques and standards for secure data access over the Internet. Such technical matters are well beyond the remit of this book. Here I am therefore only going to address the equally important but non-technical aspects of cloud computing security. As explained in the following sections, these involve adopting the safest cloud computing policies and end-user practices.

Establish a policy

I am never surprised to meet people concerned about cloud computing security. However, I continue to be staggered by the number of companies that have no cloud computing policy whatsoever! Like them or loathe them, the online software applications discussed in chapter three do exist. At the very least, every organization therefore ought to draw up and communicate to its staff a clear policy that sets out which kinds of data they are and are not allowed to work on in the cloud.

A cloud computing policy may be as simple as 'no form of company data may be uploaded, created or worked upon in Google Docs, Zoho, Acrobat.com, Microsoft Office Web Apps, or any other form of online software application'. This would hardly be a policy for effective cloud computing. However, it would at least be the start of a document that could then become more liberal as the risks and benefits were more fully assessed and understood.

It should, however, be noted that even a policy as restrictive as the above could soon prove problematic. For example, would the above policy prevent an employee from accessing, and then working, on a Google Docs file shared with them by a customer? Or by somebody working for another organization? Adopting a 'we will not cloud compute because it is not safe' policy may sound a very easy option. However, as cloud computing is a means of collaborative communication as well as data storage and processing, avoiding cloud computing entirely will not remain a viable option for very long. This strongly suggests that most organizations will rapidly need a policy that promotes safe cloud computing practices rather than no practice at all.

Ensure safe access

Most breaches in cloud computing security exploit the vulnerability of individual users and the devices they use to access the cloud. In other words, it is not the security of large cloud computing vendors, such as Google, Amazon and Microsoft, that ought to be our first concern. Rather, we should concentrate on how easy it may be for hackers to obtain illegitimately the usernames and passwords that we use to access our cloud computing accounts. As mentioned in chapter one, it is far easier to hack an individual PC than a corporate data centre.

This chapter is being written in January 2010 in the same week that the Google e-mail accounts of Chinese dissidents were allegedly hacked by the Chinese government. What most reports of this global news story suggested was that the security of Google's cloud data centres had been compromised. However, this was not the case. Rather, what is understood to have happened is that hackers exploited a security flaw in the Internet Explorer web browser that enabled them to plant spyware on the PCs of individual Chinese dissidents. These malicious or 'malware' programs then e-mailed the Google usernames and passwords of the dissidents back to the hackers. This stolen information was then used to 'legitimately' access their e-mail accounts. Some may argue that the end result was the same. However, it is very important to appreciate that security was compromised at the user and not the vendor end of the cloud computing chain.

What the above ought to tell us in spades is that anybody really concerned about cloud computing security ought to worry first and foremost about the security of their cloud access device. A company's chosen SaaS, PaaS or IaaS vendor may have the best security in the world. However, such security becomes largely irrelevant if hackers steal an employee's username and password and use them to access a company's cloud resources. In turn what this implies is that every individual and organization ought to make sure that they are accessing the web as securely as possible.

Although measures for ensuring safe web access ought to be widely known and practised, this sadly is not the case. Free sound advice is available from many websites including the UK government's getsafeonline.org. Some basic guidance is also as follows.

The first measure to take to try and ensure online security is to install and constantly update a firewall. In addition, anti-virus and anti-spyware software also needs to be installed and continuously updated to prevent key-stroke readers, viruses and other malware from infecting a computer.

Another critical measure is to ensure that the operating system and web browser on a computer are constantly updated with the latest security patches and other updates. Given that all such updates are free, it is ludicrous for anybody who uses the web – let alone who computes in the cloud – not to install them. Users of wireless networks should also ensure that they have enabled encryption to prevent others from eavesdropping on their Internet communications. However, again this is something that often does not happen, with a great many personal wireless networks remaining totally insecure.

All Internet users also need to be educated not to open suspicious e-mails that may contain and install malware. It is also critical for every user of a cloud computing resource to set a different and secure or 'strong' password for every application they use. In practical terms this means using passwords that are at least eight characters long, and that contain a mix of upper- and lower-case letters and numbers. Good passwords should also not be real words that can be found in a dictionary, related to the user, or otherwise easy to guess.

While the above is common, sound advice, there is strong evidence that it is often not heeded. For example, in January 2010 researchers at Imperva Application Defense Center did an analysis of 32 million user account passwords held by social networking application maker RockYou.com. What they discovered was that the most popular passwords were '123456', '12345', '123456789' and 'password'. Also in the top twenty were 'iloveyou', 'qwerty', 'abc123', '654321' and several common forenames. If these kinds of passwords are in more general, regular use then this has to be very bad news indeed.

Everybody ought to keep all of the passwords and any other memorable information they use to access online accounts absolutely private. This may sound a very obvious point to make. However, in many offices passwords are still written on Post-it notes stuck to monitor screens. It is also not unknown for people to base their passwords or memorable account information on favourite colours, films or places that they then also publicly list on Facebook or other social networking websites. If you happen to be guilty of this last foolish endeavour then I suggest that you change your passwords or memorable information immediately!

By taking heed of basic advice it is possible to very significantly reduce the risk of cloud computing security breaches at the user or access-device level. Unfortunately, however, computer security can only ever be as strong as the weakest link in the chain. What this means is that there is little point in maintaining high levels of security on an office PC if cloud accounts are also accessed from insecure home PCs or netbooks. This issue is also perhaps the hardest but most important for companies to address. The any-device-access aspect of cloud computing is one of its greatest benefits. However, it is also potentially a considerable drawback in security terms. Because of this we may soon start to see employers' conducting mandatory reviews of their employees' home and mobile computer security. A list of those devices that may be used to access company cloud resources ought also to be included in any cloud computing policy.

Carefully choose your vendor

While safe cloud access is probably the most major security issue, it still remains important to make a careful choice of cloud computing vendor. The most obvious move is to sign up with a big supplier, such as Google, Amazon, Microsoft, Adobe or IBM. This may make it difficult for smaller vendors to enter the growing cloud computing marketplace. However, from the customer's perspective, the most secure cloud computing vendors are likely to be those with the greatest reputations to lose.

All cloud computing vendors recognize that having a reputation for good security is likely to be a strong determinant of their failure or success. It is therefore perhaps not surprising that, in an interview with *Computer Weekly* in 2009, a Google spokesperson noted how 'security is built into the DNA of our products'. He then went on to add that 'Google practices a defence-in-depth security strategy by architecting security into our people, process and technologies'.

Assessing cloud vendor security is, in many respects, a highly technical matter. However, any business considering a move into the cloud is still well advised to ask non-technical questions. For example, it is worth determining who may have access to a vendor's data centre, and in particular whether maintenance or support is ever out-sourced to a third party. This point noted, before asking such questions a company ought to audit its own internal systems. There is after all little point in dismissing a cloud computing vendor on security grounds if access to a company's own internal data centre is currently insecure. This point is also well known to cloud computing vendors, with many now claiming that system security will be increased by adopting their services.

Consider a private or hybrid cloud

When choosing an infrastructure as a service (IaaS) vendor, companies need to consider the most appropriate type of hosting for their cloud servers. As discussed in the last chapter, there are four options available. They range from cloud hosting (when all the infrastructure is shared) to using a private cloud (when a customer rents dedicated cloud resources). All companies ideally ought to list within their cloud computing policy those types of data that they are, and are not, prepared to store and process on a shared server infrastructure. Once such a policy exists this will make their choice of cloud service far more straightforward.

Maintain local back-ups

Individuals using free cloud computing applications, such as

Google Docs, Zoho, Acrobat.com or Microsoft Web Apps, ought to consider keeping local back-ups of their files. In most cases creating such back-ups is very easy. For example, in Google Docs it takes only a few seconds to click on 'File' and 'Download as Word' to save a copy of a document to a local drive. Alternatively, Google allows users to export some or all of their documents in a single zip file up to 2Gb in size.

My own policy to prevent possible data loss is to save a local copy of every Google Docs file each time I work on it. Some people have told me that this is crazy, paranoid and negates the benefits of the cloud. Google Docs has after all never let me down and I have never had to go back to a local back-up file. However, when using a free SaaS application I feel that keeping local back-ups spread across my various cloud access devices is simply common sense. It is also a good practice for many organizations to follow provided that local back-ups are only downloaded to storage devices that are themselves fully secure.

Availability and Reliability

As mentioned at the start of this chapter, alongside security the greatest concern associated with cloud computing is the availability of a reliable service. In other words, individuals and organizations worry that they may not always have access to the cloud when they need their data and applications. It is all very well to trust that the data stored on a vendor's infrastructure will be safe. However, if access cannot always be guaranteed then cloud computing may still be considered problematic.

What any cloud computing user wants is constant access to their remote computing resources any time and anywhere. Whether this is possible will depend on both the reliability of their cloud vendor's infrastructure and the quality of each user's connection to the Internet. Once again, some responsibility has to rest with the customer, and in particular with the customer's choice of Internet service provider. However, over the next few years a reliable, high-speed Internet connection will increasingly be within reach of the majority.

Governments around the world are starting to promise a fast Internet connection for everyone, and in 2009 Finland's government even proclaimed a broadband Internet connection to be a 'human right'. In the same year, the UK's *Digital Britain* report guaranteed broadband access for everybody in the country by 2012. Developing nations are also making heavy investments in Internet infrastructure. As one of the most significant examples, in 2009 a new high-speed undersea cable connected East Africa to the rest of the Internet.

Private individuals and small companies may obtain some protection from potential Internet connection failures by purchasing multiple connection services. For example, a pay-as-you-go 3G wireless broadband dongle can be kept in reserve in case a wired broadband connection fails.

To lessen their total dependence on a constant Internet connection, some online applications are already being designed so that they can run locally if required. For example, Google now provides a plug-in called 'Google Gears' that can be added to any modern web browser. This provides Google Docs users with the option of working off-line. If this option is selected, documents are downloaded to their computer and synchronized when they are next online. This facility is great when a user knows that they are going to be without an Internet connection (for example when travelling). However, it does not protect against an unanticipated loss of Internet connectivity or an unreliable connection.

Those with a reliable, high-speed Internet connection are most likely to harbour concerns that their vendor may not be able to provide a reliable service level. Such worries are also not unfounded. In fact, vendor reliability is a manifestly larger risk for cloud computing than vendor security. All large cloud computing suppliers invest millions in hardware to try and ensure that their servers always keep running. However, it is still the case that computers fail far more regularly than they are hacked.

For all of these reasons, any company committing to a significant use of cloud resources needs to think very carefully about the implications of potential downtime. They should also compare the 'guaranteed' service levels offered by different vendors and the compensation they may receive in the event of a service failure.

Unfortunately, even the biggest cloud computing vendors do experience service outages. For example, in June 2009 Google App Engine experienced performance problems and had to go into an 'unplanned maintenance mode' which meant that developers could not update their applications. In the same month, IaaS provider Rackspace experienced a power outage at its Dallas data centre for about forty-five minutes that took many popular customer websites offline. The company suffered another short power failure the following month, affecting around 2,000 of its 60,000 customers.

Problems like these may simply be seen as early cloud computing teething troubles. However, it has to be recognized that even the best cloud vendors will very occasionally experience downtime. Typical service-level agreements (SLAs) also make this explicit. Google, for example, guarantees a 99.9 per cent up-time for the business e-mail service included in Google Apps. This means that up to ten minutes of downtime a week might be expected.

SLAs from IaaS providers tend to offer higher up-time guarantees. For example, Amazon Elastic Compute Cloud advertises a 99.95 per cent annual up-time (permitting five minutes of downtime a week). This is not bad for a cloud-hosting provider. However, GoGrid advertise a 100 per cent server up-time backed with a 10,000 per cent service failure credit. In other words, if the service is down for one hour, GoGrid provides 100 hours of free service in compensation. Whether this is a good deal depends on your line of business and point of view. It is also worth noting that RackSpace's '100% network up-time guarantee' was clearly broken twice for some of its customers due to its power failures in 2009. My own inclination is always to trust a company offering a 99-point-something up-time guarantee far more than one promising the near impossibility of a 100 per cent service level.

Ultimately, companies contemplating cloud computing need to compare the reliability of their existing internal provision with that claimed, and actually delivered, by possible cloud suppliers. When this is done, it is frequently discovered that internal systems downtime is often quite high, making the relatively low downtime of most cloud vendors actually quite attractive. Even RackSpace, with its power failures, was only down for some of its customers for less than one hour throughout the whole of 2008 and 2009. It should also be remembered that when cloud vendor services fail, fixing the issue is the vendor's problem. Once again this can be seen as an advantage, and especially so if reasonable compensation clauses are in place, or if an internal IT department does not have a strong track record for rapid fixes.

Cloud Security Advantages

As the last section started to suggest, cloud computing can have notable security and reliability advantages. Not least, having data stored in the cloud can provide a significant level of back-up that is difficult and time consuming for many users to achieve by other means. For example, as an author it is great to work on a book and not have to worry about taking a disk or USB key with me every time I leave the office. With every word written in the cloud I know that, in addition to my local back-up, my files are always secure in a Google data centre. In fact I know that my files are always secure in two data centres, as Google operates a system called synchronous replication that stores a copy of all customer data in two data centres just in case one fails. This arrangement provides a very robust level of data security that was almost impossible for a private individual to achieve a few years ago. This level of data security is now also available to everyone.

The majority of small businesses that lose all of their data in a fire, flood or burglary go out business within eighteen months. For small firms, having data securely held in a remote data centre or two is therefore potentially invaluable. To its significant credit, cloud computing can now provide all of us with the security of storing our files in the kind of large data centre that only corporates used to be able to afford. Anybody, for example, can now register with Microsoft Skydrive at skydrive.live.com and immediately start using 25Gb of free, secure online storage.

Another security advantage is that cloud computing may significantly reduce the risks of data inadvertently falling into the wrong hands. In recent years, there have been many high-profile incidents where data has been lost or stolen on laptops, CDs or USB keys left on trains or misplaced in the post. For example, in 2007 Her Majesty's Revenue and Customs (HRMC) in the UK lost the records of 15,000 Standard Life customers on a CD misplaced by a courier. In the same year, laptops stolen from two employees of Marks

& Spencer and the Nationwide Building Society contained thousands of employee and customer records. However, such security breaches were dwarfed later in the year by HRMC's loss of the bank details of 25 million people on two misplaced CDs.

Just how many USB keys disappear through the holes they wear in trouser pockets we may never know. However, what the above traditional computing horror stories ought to indicate is that cloud computing may massively decrease the likelihood of those security breaches that can result from the loss or theft of data media or entire computers. This said, great care still needs to be taken not to keep local back-ups on media and computers at high risk of theft or loss. It is also critical that users always log out after accessing cloud services on laptops, netbooks, smartphones and other mobile computing devices. This is because if such computers end up in the wrong hands, they present the possibility of unauthorized access to cloud accounts.

A final potential security benefit of cloud computing is that it may actually make personal computing much safer. As already mentioned, it is far easier to hack an individual PC than a corporate data centre. However, cloud computing developments may soon significantly increase the security of individual PCs and other computing devices. For example, Google's forthcoming Chrome OS operating system relies entirely on Google Docs and other cloud-based applications and storage. In turn, as Google are already advertising, this will make Chrome OS-based computers far more secure as it simply will not be possible for applications to be locally installed.

Given that viruses, keystroke readers and other malware are local applications, developments like Google Chrome OS are very good news indeed. Not being able to install local applications on a computer may appear restrictive. However, we ought also to see it as a positive development that will stop illegitimate others installing programs intended to compromise our security. For years we have heralded computers as programmable devices. However, in security terms the safest computing device is one that is not programmable and on which nothing can ever be installed.

Privacy and Data Protection

Computer security and reliability are basically concerned with maintaining access to data and ensuring that others do not obtain access. In addition to these critical operational imperatives, all organizations that handle personal information additionally need to be mindful of privacy and data protection issues. In most countries there are data protection laws with which anybody holding personal data needs to comply. Any organization contemplating cloud computing therefore has to ensure that its online data processing and storage is in line with relevant legislation.

In the UK, the key piece of data protection legislation is the Data Protection Act (1998). This requires the registration of all databases that contain personal information. Registrants are also required to ensure the accuracy and security of the data that they hold. In addition, all public sector organizations in the UK need to comply with the Freedom of Information Act (2005). This requires them to supply most forms of information that they hold in response to any formal request from a member of the public.

Both of the above pieces of legislation – as well as similar legislation in other countries – may lead some organizations to only use cloud computing vendors which can guarantee the geographic location of the data centre in which their information will be stored and processed. Cloud computing vendors are also starting to recognize this fact. For example, Amazon Web Services now offers customers the choice of a data centre in North Virginia, North California or Ireland.

Cloud computing also raises broader legal and privacy issues. For example, a cloud computing vendor may, on occasion, be compelled to release customer data to the police or other government agencies. This may even happen without the customer's knowledge. Whereas a company holding its own data may decide to challenge such a request, their cloud computing vendor may be far less likely to question the authorities, let alone to go to court on their behalf.

The legal and civil liberty implications of cloud computing will almost certainly only become clear after much of our data has been transferred into the cloud. Some, perhaps rightly, consider this to be hugely problematic. I will therefore return to privacy issues in the final two chapters of this book.

The Train and Plane Crash Phenomenon

As I have already mentioned, this chapter was written in the week in which some Google e-mail accounts were allegedly hacked by the Chinese government. Following this incident, the German and French governments advised their citizens not to use Microsoft Internet Explorer on security grounds. A few days later there was also an apparent glitch at AT&T that directed some customers into other people's Facebook accounts. You may therefore reasonably question why I can have any faith whatsoever in cloud computing security.

My gut reaction to the above is threefold. For a start, I would reiterate that nothing is safe and that we have to spend our lives balancing risks. Second, it is worth stressing again that cloud computing risks are massively misrepresented by a popular press that does not understand the difference between using spyware to steal passwords (which may happen fairly regularly) and hacking a cloud data centre (which certainly does not). Finally, when it comes to the reliability of the cloud, we need to consider the 'train crash phenomenon'.

Trains rarely come disastrously off the rails. In fact, rail is one of the safest ways to travel. However, train crashes that result in injuries or fatalities always make national headlines. In contrast, most road accidents that result in casualties do not get even local news coverage. This is bizarre given that, in the UK alone, around 3,000 people a year are killed on the road and on average fewer than six in rail accidents.

It is of course the infrequency and magnitude of rail disasters that makes them newsworthy in comparison to the sad regularity of fatal car accidents. However, anybody reliant on news reports to decide the safest way to travel could easily be misled. The same also applies when it comes to assessing the risks of cloud computing.

It is reasonable to guess that many tens of thousands of people suffer PC hardware failures and data loss every day. Hundreds and maybe even thousands of company servers also probably experience some downtime every week. The exact figures we will never know. Due to their regularity – and just like fatal car crashes – traditional data disasters are simply not reported.

In contrast, like train crashes, cloud data centre failures are so rare that they always receive major press attention. For example, on 13 October 2009 a server failure in a Microsoft cloud data centre was very widely reported. The problem resulted in the loss of personal information for T-Mobile customers who were using Sidekick mobile phones to store data in the Microsoft cloud. At the time of writing, this incident also remains cloud computing's greatest train crash.

In October 2009, far more people will have lost data performing traditional computing activities than computing in the cloud. However, only those who lost data due to the

Sidekick incident got reported. This may therefore have given the false impression that cloud computing is far riskier than traditional computing, which in most instances it is not. We therefore need to be mindful that the magnitude of the cloud will result in the press over-emphasizing its errors or 'train crashes', even though such problems will be far rarer than in non-cloud situations. It is also worth noting that by 15 October 2009 all 'lost' Sidekick data had been recovered (an inconvenient truth that was not widely reported). I would also place a fairly safe bet that all of those other people in the world who lost data on 13 October 2009 had not got it back by the 15th and that most of them never did.

* * *

Wading in Blood So Deep

In the third act of William Shakespeare's *Macbeth*, the title character laments how he has waded in blood so deeply that he might as well continue on. I do not really want to compare cloud computing to a murderous tyrant. However, I would suggest that those who oppose the cloud on security grounds could learn a thing or two from the aforementioned Scottish king. Many of those who bemoan the potential risks of cloud computing are avid web users. It is therefore rather strange that they appear oblivious to the fact that we have long since mortgaged our souls to the Internet.

Ever since we began attaching documents to e-mails we have been trusting our data to the cloud. In fact, creating and sharing a spreadsheet with Google Docs is almost certainly safer than creating it in Microsoft Excel and exchanging it as an e-mail attachment. This is because, when a document is created in an SaaS application, trust only has to be placed in one cloud vendor. In contrast, each time an e-mail attachment is exchanged, trust has to be placed in both the sender's and the recipient's e-mail provider. Whenever we send somebody a document attached to an e-mail we also have to trust that they will download and store it securely. In contrast, a document shared in the cloud may never be downloaded to another computer. When a document is shared using an SaaS application rather than attached to an e-mail, the sender can also decide whether the recipient has the right to view-and-edit the file or just view it. Once again we see the potential security benefits of cloud computing.

Like typing a credit card number into a website, cloud computing is something that the majority of us will sooner rather than later simply accept and stop worrying about. As I have noted repeatedly in this chapter, our biggest fear ought really to be the security of the computing devices we use to access the cloud, rather than the security, reliability and trustworthiness of cloud vendors. The fact that so many of us still do not take enough basic online security precautions is therefore the thing that we most need to address.

A more mature understanding of security issues is likely to fuel the demand for cloud access devices that are extremely difficult to infiltrate. As this demand rises, there may well also be a wider realization that because the cloud is programmable, our own computers do not have to be. This may in turn lead to a whole host of new and very secure computer hardware on to which it is nigh-on impossible for hackers to download spyware and other malicious code. New forms of cloud access device are also what the next chapter is all about.

6

THE SECOND DIGITAL REVOLUTION

However much I enthuse about it in this book, very few people will ever care about the cloud. They won't take it for walks, send it a birthday card, or ever invite it on holiday. This is also hardly surprising for two reasons. The first is that the cloud is not, at least yet, a sentient entity that any sane person ought to care about. The second is that the vast data centres of computer hardware that make up the cloud are far removed from most people's everyday lives.

The above is absolutely as it should be. Human beings live and love, reproduce and die, in the real, physical world. In contrast, the cloud is an artificial, virtual realm sometimes referred to as 'cyberspace'. For the cloud to have a real impact on our everyday human activities, it therefore needs a very effective interface to the real world. The continuing development of that interface – of those myriad items of computer hardware that allow us to interact with the cloud – is therefore what this chapter is all about.

The First Digital Revolution
The birth of personal computing in the late 1970s kick-started our addiction to all things digital. The IBM PC was launched in the US in 1981, and by the middle of the 1980s

the First Digital Revolution had well and truly begun. Within both offices and homes, personal computers were increasingly used to work on documents, spreadsheets and databases. They were also starting to be booted up to draw and process images, to help compose and record music, and to play first-generation computer games.

Along with early personal computing, the First Digital Revolution was heavily focused around 'digitization'. What this means is that most First Digital Revolution developments involved the transformation of physical things into digital content that could be stored, manipulated and accessed on a computer. By the 1990s, digitization had extended to documents, most forms of company data, photographs, books, newspapers, music and video. Amazing as it may seem, it is around two decades since most media began to be pushed into cyberspace or what we now term 'the cloud'.

Twenty years ago it was possible to use a computer to read a book, look at photographs, listen to music, or watch a video. However, very few people actually did so. Partly this was because computers capable of storing and processing high-resolution images, audio and video were very expensive. However, the other major restriction was that the only kinds of devices that could be used to access cyberspace were desktop PCs. What this meant was that consumers of early digital media were pretty much restricted to their desks.

One of the reasons that cloud computing is now starting to take hold is that we are in the early days of the Second Digital Revolution. While the first was concerned with digitization and personal computers, the second involves 'atomization' and 'ubiquitous computing'.

Atomization is the reverse of digitization, and occurs when digital content is turned back into atoms in a form that we can see, hear or touch. Ubiquitous computing therefore concerns the development of those non-traditional computing devices that facilitate atomization. For example, iPods and digital photo frames are both ubiquitous computing devices. They can be described this way because iPods allow us to listen to music anywhere, while digital photo frames permit digital pictures to be displayed on our mantelpieces.

The Second Digital Revolution will increasingly free people from having to use a PC or laptop if they want to access the cloud. In essence, all of its developments are intended to make digital things accessible via atomization. In contrast, most First Digital Revolution developments were focused on putting real things into computers via digitization. The concepts of digitization, atomization and the First and Second Digital Revolutions are brought together in figure 6.1.

The Rise of Ubiquitous Computing

By the middle of the 1990s, most analysts were predicting that the Next Big Thing in computing would be virtual reality. Daily forays were predicted into incredible virtual worlds that people would inhabit for work and play. Much research therefore went into developing 3D glasses and 'head-mounted displays' (HMDs) that people were expected to wear to gain access to a virtual reality Internet. However, as you may have noticed, mainstream virtual reality never took hold.

You may be wondering why computer scientists and futurists around fifteen years ago got it so wrong. The answer is two-fold. First, few people foresaw the extent to which most of us would be happy to communicate online using traditional computer screens. So, in a sense, virtual reality did arrive. It just happened to materialize in two

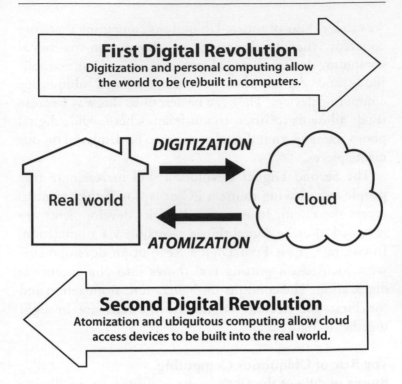

Figure 6.1: The First and Second Digital Revolutions

dimensions in the form of popular social networking sites like Facebook, MySpace and Twitter.

The second reason why predictions of a 3D virtual reality future were wrong is more technical. In the 1990s, computer scientists did know that there were two possible ways that computing could develop. One was virtual reality, which in essence involved building new worlds within computers. The second was ubiquitous computing, which involved building loads of new types of computer into the real world.

Ubiquitous computing was first developed in the Palo Alto Research Center (PARC) labs of Rank Xerox from 1988 to 1994. The basic premise of taking digital content to people – rather than requiring people to go to a PC to access digital content – was almost instantly appreciated as being very powerful. However, back in the 1990s, the idea of building loads of computers into the real world seemed far more problematic than the virtual reality challenge of building new worlds within computers.

What most people in the 1990s thought would kill ubiquitous computing dead was its massive range of new technology requirements. For a start, revolutionary screen, microprocessor and battery technologies were needed if powerful computers were going to be mobile and even carried in our pockets. Widespread, high-speed wireless networking was also required, which in the days of dial-up Internet access seemed like a luxurious pipe dream. For ubiquitous computing to really work, people also needed to be able to access their data from any device. In other words, in addition to screen, microprocessor, battery and wireless networking innovations that were all destined to be delivered, ubiquitous computing also required a large proportion of our data and applications to be in the cloud.

The Device Cloud

Today, the stage is set for ubiquitous computing to come of age. This means that we will increasingly be able to access digital content and applications anywhere and anyhow we want. You can already see this happening, with many of us carrying first-generation ubiquitous computing devices, such as mobile phones and digital music players. Second-generation ubiquitous computing devices are also rapidly starting to arrive. These have full Internet connectivity, and enable a more complete atomization of the cloud back into our everyday lives.

Figure 6.2 illustrates the emerging 'device cloud'. This is a representation of the array of ubiquitous computing

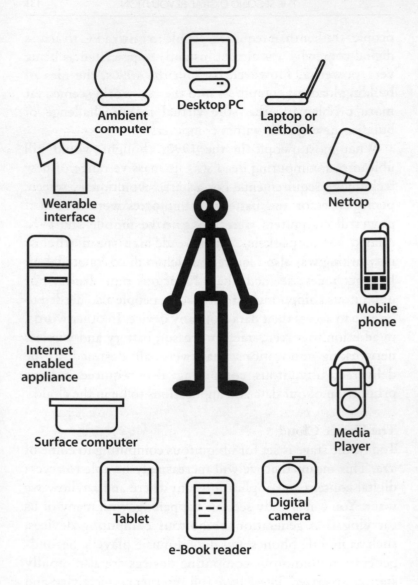

Figure 6.2: The device cloud

devices that can allow us to access all of our cloud data and applications when, where and how we choose. Some of these devices you will recognize , while others are likely to be new to you as technologies that are only just emerging on the market. However, what all forms of hardware in the device cloud have in common is their ability to turn digital data into something that we can see, hear or touch.

The following sections detail the twelve categories of computing device illustrated in the device cloud. However, perhaps the most important point to appreciate is that none of them is being presented as an alternative. While back in the nineties and noughties most people had access to only one or two computers, in the near future this will no longer be the case. Rather, it will be normal for most of us to regularly use a great many different devices to access the cloud.

Desktop PCs

Ten years ago many people tried to convince me that the desktop computer was a dinosaur that would soon become extinct. This was not true then and it is not true today. For those many computing activities that require extended periods of high concentration, we will be using desktop PCs for a long time to come. However, with our applications, data and processor power increasingly out in the cloud, most of those big boxes on or under our desks are likely to disappear. This is because all of the processor power we need locally will be able to be embedded in our keyboard units or screens.

Laptops and netbooks

Having said that desktop computers will be around for a long time, laptops and netbooks are already providing very stiff competition. Many laptops are now as well specified as some desktops. They also have the advantage of coming in a nice, portable form-factor that can warm your thighs on a chilly evening if you do not own a cat.

Netbooks are basically cut-down laptops with typically a nine-, ten- or eleven-inch screen and a reasonable if not full-size keyboard. While the first netbook was produced by Psion in 2000, it was the launch of the Eee PC range from Asus in late 2007 that made netbooks a mass-market phenomenon. One of the main reasons for the Eee's success was a price tag of £200–300, depending on the model. As other manufacturers raced to launch their own netbooks, they had no choice but to match this price point despite the significant impact on their profit margins. Today, netbooks account for about 20 per cent (and rising) of the laptop market. In fact, in 2009 revenue from netbooks doubled to $11.7bn globally against the background of the continuing recession and stagnant desktop and laptop sales.

Most netbooks are now based on a microprocessor from Intel called the Atom. This makes them very energy efficient, so extending battery life. In turn this means that netbooks are far more environmentally friendly than a traditional laptop or desktop computer. A typical netbook user will burn 20–30 watts of power an hour, compared to the 60–75 watts of a typical laptop, or the 100-plus watts of most desktop PCs.

In the next chapter I will examine the launch of the Google Chrome operating system that will further drive the growth of the netbook market. This new cloud-based competitor to Microsoft Windows is being targeted specifically at netbooks, and is being built from the ground up to run on low-power computers with all applications accessed online.

Nettops
Take a netbook, rip off the screen and add an HDMI socket

to connect it to your television, and you have a nettop. This may sound simplistic, but it is basically true. Nettop computers take components, such as Intel's low-energy Atom processor, and put them in the living room to allow us access to the web on our televisions. As more and more video content is available online, so the nettop market is also likely to expand significantly.

Current nettop models include the Asus Eee Box, the Zoostorm and the Acer Aspire Revo. Similar cut-down and energy-saving 'thin client' computers are also starting to be used in businesses, including those provided by ThinDesk.com.

Many nettops can be bolted to the back of a monitor or television. This therefore begs the question of whether nettop computing functions will eventually be integrated into many televisions, so removing the need for a separate computing device. Either way, accessing media content and cloud computing applications on a television is likely to be very common within five years.

Mobile phones

The mobile phone has already become the first mass-adopted ubiquitous computing device. In fact, it may not be long before most people in developed nations carry with them a sophisticated, online mobile phone – or 'smartphone' – that allows them to browse the web, run cloud applications and play media content in addition to sending texts and making a call. For some people, a smartphone with a reasonable-size screen and a decent Internet connection is already the only cloud computing hardware that they really need. For others, their iPhone, Blackberry, Windows Mobile or Android handset is an excellent and essential mobile complement to their desktop or laptop computer.

Media players

Saehan Information Systems and Diamond Multimedia produced the first mass-market MP3 music players in the late 1990s. However, it was the launch of the first Apple iPods in 2001 that got the media player market moving. Today, devices from Apple, Archos, Creative, Sony and many others allow us to carry a great deal of digital audio and video in our pockets. Some of the latest devices even allow digital content to be accessed directly over the Internet, or wirelessly from a home computer network. We should therefore increasingly expect to use media players to access online music and video, as well as cloud applications.

Digital cameras

The final piece of traditional hardware in the device cloud is the digital camera. However, with many other gadgets (including mobile phones and netbooks) now having an integrated camera, the market for stand-alone consumer cameras may increasingly be squeezed. In response to this, wireless Internet connectivity is starting to be incorporated. This enables, for example, a digital camera to take a picture and upload it directly to a photo-sharing website. Given that many digital cameras now have screens at least as large as some mobile phones and media players, cameras with a built-in web browser are also a significant possibility.

e-Book readers

During 2008 and 2009, e-book readers entered the fray as a new kind of device for accessing digital content downloaded from the Internet. E-book readers – sometimes just called e-readers – are computing devices about the size of a traditional book and feature an e-ink display. These provide a paper-like reading experience due to their high contrast and resolution. E-ink screens are also very power efficient as current is only used to change rather than maintain the image. Given that the screen or page on an e-book reader is only turned/changed relatively infrequently, this allows many days and even weeks of reading from a single battery charge.

Several e-book readers are now on the market. The most famous is the Kindle from Amazon, already in its second generation. As Amazon describe, this is as thin as most magazines, readable in direct sunlight, can download a book in sixty seconds, and stores up to 1,500 or 3,500 books, depending on the model. Alternatives include the Sony Reader, BeBook and the QUE ProReader from Plastic Logic. The latter is particularly interesting as its 10.7-inch shatterproof display is manufactured from a new kind of flexible, plastic electronics. The first 'dualbook' – a combination e-book reader and netbook in one – is now also available from enTourage. Its eDGe device opens up with a 9.7-inch e-ink screen on one side and a 10.1-inch screen on the other. This allows it to handle all kinds of digital media and offer full netbook and e-book reader functions.

E-book readers are unlikely ever to replace traditional books. However, many commentators predict that e-book readers or tablets will change the face of newspaper, magazine and non-fiction publishing. Most newspapers are now struggling financially in the face of free online content, and charging a subscription to have their publication delivered from the cloud to an e-book reader is an attractive new business model. New opportunities will also involve subscriptions being offered for part of a publication. In the near future we may even be able to customize our own newspaper by mashing the sports section of one newspaper with the arts and entertainment section of another.

Tablets

With the launch of the much-hyped Apple iPad in January 2010, the computer industry once again caught tablet fever. This first happened in November 2002 when Microsoft launched the TabletPC edition of Windows XP. At that time, many notable PC manufacturers, including Toshiba and Compaq, went on to build tablet PCs to Microsoft's TabletPC specification. However, back in the early noughties, tablets never really caught the public imagination.

A tablet is basically a laptop/netbook computer without a keyboard and operated by a touch screen. Back in the Microsoft TabletPC days, tablets were single-touch, operated with a stylus, and as large as most laptops. However, devices like the iPad are a whole new breed of far slimmer, lighter computers with multi-touch interfaces operated by our fingers. While first-generation tablets were mainly intended to run locally installed applications, this time around tablets are being acclaimed as interfaces to the cloud.

Apple's iPad is basically a very large iPod touch, and indeed runs the same operating system as Apple's highly successful smartphone. In competition, Microsoft has teamed up with HP to create a new tablet or 'slate PC' that runs Windows 7. Also launched in January 2010, this is multi-touch like the iPad, and is also intended to be used to access the web and play digital media. Not far behind, Google has indicated its intention to launch a tablet device that will run its Chrome OS operating system. Veteran media player manufacturer Archos has also already got a Windows 7 tablet on the market in the form of its rather stylish, Atom-based Archos 9 Tablet PC.

Tablets are expected to compete head-on with e-book readers to become the most popular devices that people will use to access digital books, newspapers, magazines and other documents. Currently e-book readers have the advantage of clearer if black-and-white e-ink screens, as well as a better battery life. On the other hand, tablets have the benefit of colour screens and offer pretty much full web access. Tablets also provide the opportunity to run SaaS applications, which may well give them the advantage. We shall see!

Surface computers

Surface computers provide an interface similar to that of an extremely large tablet that has been embedded into a wall, tabletop or other surface. The computer display is projected on to the surface, which then also functions as a multi-touch screen. Using their fingers on the surface, users can launch applications, drag media objects around, and zoom in and out of photographs, maps and videos.

One of the first surface computers was a coffee-table-size piece of hardware called Microsoft Surface. This is already in commercial use in some hotel lobbies, clubs and restaurants, and uses cameras below the table top to recognize objects placed on it. The integrated wireless connectivity then helps provide a quite spectacular integration of the real and digital worlds.

For example, if a mobile phone is placed on Microsoft Surface, any images taken with its camera will spread out around it on the table. If a second phone is then placed down, a finger can be used to drag selected images from one phone to the other. In a restaurant, payment can be made by dragging items from an onscreen bill to one or more credit cards placed on the surface. Videos can also be mapped to appear on clear glass squares that can be moved around on the surface like pieces in a video jigsaw.

Surface computing has currently only been seen by most people in films like *Minority Report* in which Tom Cruise manipulated data on the wall before him with his fingers.

However, with advances in nanotechnology, it may one day become possible to create smart paints that will allow any surface to become a surface computer. When and if that happens, ubiquitous computing could take a giant leap forward, with cloud interfaces integrated all around us in our homes, offices and public spaces.

Internet-enabled appliances

Another ubiquitous computing trend is for the integration of computer power and Internet connectivity in domestic appliances. The result could be a world in which many everyday objects will allow us to access the cloud. Some objects may even go online all by themselves.

Back in the noughties, one of the most oft-cited Internet-enabled appliances was the Internet fridge. The idea was that such appliances would read the RFID tags or bar codes on food to keep track of what was inside them. In theory, this would have allowed an Internet fridge to make diet and recipe suggestions, and to automatically order new food supplies. The Internet fridge door was even promoted as the perfect place for family members to leave e-mails and video messages for each other.

Electrolux, LG and Samsung have all recently sold an Internet fridge. However, none of them has fulfilled its promise because they have basically been traditional fridges with an early tablet computer sunk into the door. However, interest in online appliances is growing again as electricity networks get smarter and merge with the cloud. This may in turn allow appliances to purchase their own electricity on an hourly basis from the cheapest supplier.

Already GE sells a 'demand-response refrigerator' that downloads peak-time price signals from its energy supplier. These are then used to decide the best times of day to make ice or run a defrost cycle. As energy prices rise, we should expect ever more appliances to make use of the cloud to optimize their energy efficiency and barter for the cheapest source of power.

Wearable interfaces

In the near future, interfaces to the cloud may also be routinely worn on the body. Already Zypad have developed a computer that can be worn on the forearm. Within a decade, flexible screen technologies are also likely to allow computers to be integrated into clothing. We may therefore soon be able to watch YouTube videos on our chests or scroll Google maps on our cuffs!

Other forays into wearable computing include the recently launched 'airmouse' from the Canadian firm Deanmark. This provides the functions of a traditional computer rodent, except it is worn like a glove. A group of researchers at the Virginia Polytechnic Institute are even developing a fabric with embedded sensors that may allow a pair of jeans to record the movement of the wearer's legs. The London-based fashion company CuteCircuit is also developing a number of items of interactive clothing, some of which are already on sale.

One product from CuteCircuit is the Hug Shirt. This uses an Internet connection to allow the user to send a hug to someone they love. The wearer of one Hug Shirt wraps their arms around themselves, so pressing on sensors that transmit data via their mobile phone to the wearer of a second Hug Shirt. Pads in the second Hug Shirt then exert pressure on the wearer, hence giving the impression that they are actually being remotely hugged. In theory, hugs may be stored up in the cloud for download on demand!

Ambient computers

Whereas traditional computing devices demand our

attention, ambient computers operate at the periphery of our perception. This allows them to deliver datacasts from the Internet that are less obtrusive and more comfortably integrated into the real world. A desktop PC, netbook or tablet requires its user to be looking at it to access the latest information. In contrast, ambient computing devices gradually bring information to their user's attention in a far more subtle manner.

Examples of ambient computers include clocks and devices of a similar size that are fed online information on topics including the weather, sports scores and share prices. More radical devices include the Ambient Orb and Ambient Umbrella from AmbientDevices.com.

The Ambient Orb is a six-inch frosted glass ball that gradually glows different colours to display real-time data sourced from the Internet. The Orb can be linked to all kinds of information sources, including traffic congestion on the user's route home, pollen forecasts, wind speed or the electricity consumption in part of a factory. As a review by *Time Magazine* enthusiastically explains:

> The Ambient Orb may look like a crystal ball on acid, but it's really more of a giant mood ring – plugged straight into the fluctuations of the stock market or anything else you care to track. The orb can be wirelessly configured to track any individual stock, any market index or your personal portfolio. This makes getting information a 'glanceable' thing.

The Ambient Umbrella is a computer peripheral for keeping the rain off. The idea is that it hangs in its owner's hall, constantly monitoring the weather using data from AccuWeather.com. Most of the time the umbrella is ignored. However, if the umbrella discovers that it is likely to be raining that evening, its handle will flash to remind its owner to take it with them. The Ambient Umbrella is probably the first cloud computing device to be linked to real clouds!

Augmented Reality

All of the hardware in the device cloud can be used to bring digital content into the real world. However, to link cyberspace and physical reality successfully will take more than new computing devices. In tandem, it will also require new types of application. The first of these has now also arrived in the form of augmented reality (AR).

AR overlays data from the cloud on a real-time view of the physical world. This means that a user can hold up a smartphone or tablet and see information overlaid on people, buildings or other objects viewed through its camera. Whereas the virtual reality of the First Digital Revolution required the building of new worlds inside computers for us to visit, the AR of the Second Digital Revolution will allow us to experience real and virtual reality simultaneously in everyday locations.

AR is viewed in a special web browser application. Two of these – called Layar and the Wikitude World Browser – can already be downloaded to run on the latest Apple iPhones, as well as several smartphones that run Google's Android or Nokia's Symbian operating systems. The Samsung Galaxy also had the distinction of being the first smartphone to come with the Layar AR browser pre-installed. Around 200,000 handsets are expected to be running augmented reality browsers by 2012. On 15 February 2010 the AR market also took a major leap forward when Layar made it possible for other companies to sell AR experiences on its platform.

Both Layar and the Wikitude World Browser take a smartphone's GPS and compass data and use it to work out where the handset is and what it is being pointed at. They then obtain relevant additional information from the cloud and overlay it on the phone's video feed in real-time. This allows, for example, people to point their phones at hotels and instantly see how many rooms are available and at what price. Or they can learn more about a local landmark just by pointing their phone at it.

When combined with image recognition, AR will allow information to be overlaid on any person or product. For example, hold up a smartphone in a meeting and everybody's latest tweet or YouTube video may appear to float above their head on its AR display. Alternatively, the products viewed on supermarket shelves may appear with nutrition or allergy information superimposed.

The above examples may sound rather far-fetched. However, Google has already launched a service for Android mobile phones called Google Goggles. This is a visual search application that takes still or video images and transmits them to image-recognition software in a Google data centre. Relevant information is then sent back to the phone in real-time.

Cloud computing is essential for the development of all types of augmented reality. Not least this is because the kinds of data we will want overlaid on the world will need to be aggregated from a great many sources. Visual search applications will also require large and centralized image banks and artificial intelligence systems that are constantly updated and 'taught' by all of our devices and interactions.

For business, augmented reality is likely to become a key cloud computing frontier. Early adopters will obtain good publicity, while in time more and more people will expect a company's products and services to be visible in AR. Several software developers are therefore already wading in to the embryonic augmented reality marketplace.

Just one AR pioneer is AugmentReality.co.uk. The company has already built several very interesting Layar applications. These include Layar Local Search, which helps people to locate restaurants, plumbers or other services. Some of their other applications have even started to make use of Layar's ability to integrate 3D objects into live camera feeds. For example, an application has been created that overlays virtual 3D representations of The Beatles on the zebra crossing in Abbey Road, and with whom you can even be photographed! AugmentReality.co.uk has also developed an application that allows visitors to Rotterdam to see a final version of its incomplete Provast market hall by simply pointing their phone at its construction site.

According to a report from Juniper Research in January 2010, the annual number of mobile downloads featuring augmented reality content is expected to rise from fewer than one million in 2009 to more than 400 million by 2014. Even people and organizations who ignore online software and hardware should therefore think twice before dismissing augmented reality.

3D Printing

While augmented reality may provide an increasingly effective means of manifesting the cloud in the real world, it is not the only technology pushing the barriers of atomization. Philosophically we could debate whether overlaying virtual reality on a camera feed really is a means of transforming digital information into a physical, atom-based format. However, there can be no doubt that this is exactly what 3D printing achieves.

3D printers do what their name implies. That is, they take digital data and turn it into real, solid objects. Just as an inkjet printer can turn pictures from a digital camera into 2D hardcopy prints, so a 3D printer takes a digital 3D model or scan and creates a real, physical object.

Current 3D printers use additive technologies that build up objects in layers over several hours. The first commercial 3D printer was invented by Charles Hull in 1984, and used a technique called stereolithography. This positions a perforated platform just below the surface of a vat of liquid photocurable polymer. A laser beam then traces the first slice of an object on the surface of the liquid, causing a very thin layer to harden. The perforated platform is then lowered very slightly and another slice is traced out and hardened by the laser. Another slice is then created, and then another, until a complete object has been printed.

Other commercial 3D printers use a large number of nozzles that spray droplets of hot thermoplastic to build up the slices of a final object. Yet others use a laser to fuse solid layers from a cocktail of powdered wax, ceramics, metal or nylon. There are also powder-based systems that spray a binder solution to solidify the different layers of an object. Manufacturers of 3D printers include Fortus, 3D Systems, Solid Scape, ZCorp and Desktop Factory.

Most current 3D printers are used to rapidly prototype new product designs, to output models or to make moulds that will in turn be used to produce final items. Such printers have already allowed engineers to check the fit of different parts long before they commit to costly production. Architects have also been able to show detailed scale models to their clients, while medical professionals and archae-ologists have been able to handle full-size copies of bones printed from 3D scan data. The range of consumer products that have employed 3D printers in their design process or to produce final moulds has so far included automobiles, trainers, jewellery, toys, coffee makers and all sorts of plastic bottles, packaging and containers. Dentists are now also starting to use 3D printers in the production of dental appliances.

The use of 3D printing to manufacture end-use parts is also starting to occur. For example, Fortus already sells 3D printers to allow the 'direct digital manufacturing' (DDM) of final plastic components. For low-volume manufacturing this is more cost effective than traditional methods, and allows rapid design changes and just-in-time inventory. Fortus customer Klock Werks Kustom Cycles now builds special, one-off motorcycles using a 3D printer to digitally manufacture some of the final, custom parts. Another company using 3D printing to create final products is Freedom of Creation, whose designer range includes lighting, furniture, trays, bags, jewellery and headphones.

Developments are also now occurring in 3D organ printing. Also known as bioprinting, this is where a 3D printer builds up replacement body parts using layers of cells. The US National Science Foundation has funded a multi-disciplinary 3D organ printing project in anticipation of the incredible possibilities that this may offer to create synthetic replacement organs to individual patient specification. In March 2008, 3D organ printing pioneer Organovo managed to create blood vessels and cardiac tissue using a printer that dispenses cells instead of ink. The material so created fused into living tissue just seventy hours after being printed out. Twenty hours after that it even started beating! In February 2010 Organovo then became the first company to take delivery of a production model 3D bio-printer.

3D printing is right at the cutting edge of the Second Digital Revolution. This is because it totally and utterly atomizes digital content back into the real world. 3D printing may not yet be a direct cloud computing technology. However, cloud computing and 3D printing are destined to become highly interlinked as 3D printers enter the device cloud as another form of hardware capable of atomizing digital data.

* * *

Our Life in the Cloud

As we have seen in earlier chapters, the cloud is becoming a digital realm in which individuals and organizations will store and process more and more varieties of data. New forms of computing device like those covered in this chapter will therefore continue to drive cloud computing. In turn, the increased uptake of cloud computing will continue to lead to the innovation of new categories of computer hardware.

Good access to the cloud will allow more and more physical items to be stored online in a digital format. Already photographs have gone digital, with most of us now happy to view and exchange images without resorting to hardcopy. Audio and video are also increasingly being purchased as digital downloads, with fewer of us stockpiling a library of tapes or disks in plastic cases.

By the middle of this decade, augmented reality is likely to be mainstream. In turn this will drive more and more companies to try and get their products as visible in augmented reality as they already are on the traditional world wide web. By the time this occurs, 3D printing may also be employed far more widely. If this proves to be the case, then we may store not just documents, images, audio and video in the cloud, but also physical goods, spare parts and even replacement human organs. Why have Amazon ship a product if you can download it for printout on a desktop 3D printer?

The development of augmented reality and 3D printing will further fuel the intense Battle for the Cloud. It is one thing for the cloud data centres owned by Google, Microsoft, Apple, Amazon, IBM and others to be virtually piled high with traditional digital content. However, it is quite another if they also start to fill up with augmented realities that we roam through every day, not to mention designer products and spare parts for all manner of things, including ourselves. As we will explore in the next chapter, the Battle for the Cloud is therefore a very important battle indeed.

7

THE BATTLE FOR THE CLOUD

For most of us the cloud is where we will increasingly store our data and run applications. However, for Google, Microsoft, Apple, Amazon, IBM, Oracle and other giants of the computer industry, the cloud is the new corporate battleground. There can be little doubt that those companies that control the cloud will dominate the future of computing. This chapter therefore looks at the Battle for the Cloud now being fought out within the computing industry.

Just before you consider skipping ahead to chapter eight, it is worth remembering that those companies that win the Battle for the Cloud will not only control computing. Far more importantly, they may also have a major influence over most of our lives.

Computing is already a significant aspect of the human condition, with many people conducting their personal and business affairs online. The companies that control the cloud may therefore be able to at least partially direct how we communicate and behave. As noted at the end of the last chapter, the victors in the Battle for the Cloud may also have a significant control over a wide spectrum of resources stored digitally and purchased from their vast data centres.

To appreciate what is going on in the computing industry today it is important to set current events in their historical context. Not least this will remind us that the Battle for the Cloud is not without precedent. The computing industry has always been subject to game-changing innovation and cut-throat competition. The only things that have ever changed have been the battle lines.

From Hardware to Software

Pretty much every early computing innovation was hardware based. The very first electronic computer – the ENIAC – was built in 1945 at the University of Pennsylvania. This mighty machine was constructed from 18,000 vacuum tubes. It also drew so much power that the lights of Philadelphia are reported to have dimmed when it was turned on!

ENIAC fulfilled the single purpose of calculating ballistics tables for the US Army. Software did therefore not enter the frame until 1949 when a team at Cambridge University built EDSAC, the world's first stored-program computer. The first commercial computers then soon arrived on the scene. These famously included the UNIVAC, which in 1951 became the first computer to process a United States census. A few years later Lyons Electronic Office or 'LEO' processed the payroll for a chain of tea houses.

Computing entered its second generation when transistors replaced bulky and unreliable vacuum tubes. The first such computer – the TX-0 – was completed at the Massachusetts Institute of Technology in 1958. Around this time, the first commercial programming languages were also introduced. These included the common business oriented language (COBOL), which was significant because it enabled people who were not skilled mathematicians to write software.

In the mid-1960s, computing took another major leap forward with the development of the integrated circuit. This also remains the most significant computer hardware development to this day. While first-generation computers had been built from single valves, and second-generation machines from individual transistors, integrated circuits used photographic methods to etch multiple transistors upon silicon layers that became known as microchips. While the first microchips contained only a few hundred transistors, they catapulted forward the computing revolution. In particular they allowed IBM to launch its System 360 mainframe on 7 April 1964.

In only four weeks, the IBM System 360 generated over $1bn in orders. For the first time computers therefore started to become common in business. In 1971, integrated circuit manufacturer Intel then changed the world yet again when it created the first commercial microprocessor. Named simply the '4004', this packed all of the basic components at the heart of a computer on to a single component.

Companies large and small rapidly embraced the Intel 4004 to build the first microcomputers. Suddenly computers were not only monolithic mainframes in air-conditioned buildings, but also personal desktop devices. The very first microcomputer was the Altair 8800, which was released as a kit in 1975. Ready-built personal computers were subsequently mass-marketed by Apple in 1977 and Radio Shack in 1978. IBM then gave birth to the IBM PC in 1981.

The IBM PC was a significant milestone for two reasons. For a start it was a personal computer from IBM, the company that businesses already trusted to supply their mainframes. Secondly, the hardware design of the IBM PC was open, meaning that other computer manufacturers were allowed to freely copy it. This was fantastic news for an industry populated by literally scores of totally incompatible PCs that could not easily exchange data, let alone run the same programs. At a stroke IBM therefore changed the computing landscape by creating a hardware standard that most manufacturers rapidly adhered to and most customers wanted to buy. However, IBM's clever move also handed the baton of power in the computing industry over to those who wrote the software.

From Software to Data

When IBM launched its personal computer in 1981, it chose a little-known software house to write it an operating system. That software house had been founded a few years earlier by a college drop-out called Bill Gates. His company went by the name of Microsoft.

In addition to supplying IBM, Gates aggressively marketed his MS-DOS operating system to all of the manufacturers of clone IBM PCs. This strategy was also strategically brilliant. In particular, it provided a very effective foundation for the launch of the first version of Microsoft Windows in 1985, followed by the first version of Microsoft Office in 1989. As the supplier of Windows and Office, by the early 1990s Microsoft began to rapidly displace its competitors to become the dominant player in the computing industry.

Until at least the mid-1990s, Microsoft focused almost exclusively on selling Windows and personal computing applications. However, at the time more and more people were starting to take notice of a growing phenomenon called the Internet. The birth of our planetary computer network dates back to the interlinking of various military and educational systems in the 1960s. However, it was not until the 1990s that private citizens and then business started to take a serious interest. In particular, the invention of the world wide web by Tim Berners-Lee in 1991 really kick-started the online revolution.

Initially, the world wide web consisted only of text documents connected via hyperlinks. However, this rapidly changed with the development of graphical web browsers such as Mosaic, which was launched in 1993. Around this time the Internet had fewer than two million users and only 0.1 per cent of its traffic was web based. However, as we all now know, this was about to rapidly change.

Microsoft launched its Internet Explorer web browser in 1995. By this time Mosaic had taken a 90 per cent market share under the new name of Netscape Navigator. The so-termed browser wars subsequently ensued. In these Microsoft was also triumphant, itself gaining a 90 per cent market share by 2005, with Netscape Navigator sadly reduced to less than 1 per cent.

Microsoft gained a lion's share of the browser market by including Internet Explorer with every copy of Windows. In doing so, it also engaged in a number of practices whose potentially anti-competitive nature is still causing ripples around the globe. However, while Microsoft did manage to get most of us to use its browser to get online, it nevertheless failed to fully appreciate the impact of the Internet.

The browser wars were all about getting people to install and run a particular software application to access the web. Microsoft was victorious because it arranged for most new computers to be delivered with Internet Explorer already installed. However, what both Microsoft and Netscape failed to appreciate was that as the web went mainstream, most people would not care which software they ran. Instead, the majority became far more interested in what they did when they actually got online. The road to Internet success was therefore left wide open for companies that did not want us to install anything at all.

For most people today, digital content – coupled with mechanisms for locating and working with that content – are more important than hardware or software. To date, the company that has most capitalized on this new reality has been Google. Unlike Microsoft, Google has rarely tried to get us to install anything. Instead, Google's advertised mission has always been to 'organize the world's information and make it universally accessible and useful'.

Cloud Frontiers

Within only a few years, cloud computing has thrown all of the traditional values of the computing industry into the air. Nobody yet knows what the new digital landscape will look like, let alone which companies will dominate it. However, we do know the territory that is being fought over. Before we delve further into a discussion of the most significant contenders in the Battle for the Cloud, we should therefore take stock of cloud computing's four key frontiers.

The software frontier

As already discussed several times in this book, in many ways cloud computing is making software less and less important. Increasingly, most people will focus on what they want to do with a computer, not the applications they use to help them achieve things. This said, while software will become transparent to most users, in the computer industry a great deal of power will continue to be wielded by those companies that provide our operating systems and future online applications.

A large proportion of the computing industry currently supports itself by selling software. While most companies may now recognize the inevitability of cloud computing, in the short term they still have an incentive to try and wring the last remaining profits from traditional software sales. In the past, battles on the software frontier were won by setting standards, such as the 'doc and 'xls' file formats used by Microsoft Office. However, such wars are now pretty much over, with all contenders using common file formats.

Software battles have also traditionally been fought out over features. However, with Microsoft Office and most traditional software having bloated to such a level that they are feature-rich but value-blind, future battles over features are less likely. Complex, traditional software applications will survive as niche product. However, most users are likely to flock towards simple, reliable online applications that will just let them get the job done and often collaboratively.

Within ten years the software applications we will use most of the time will be practically invisible, with the divide between using an application and using any other form of website increasingly blurred. In part this will be because all applications will be highly mashable. Already, one of the great things about the spreadsheets, charts and forms created using Google Docs, Zoho or Acrobat.com is that they can be embedded into any website. Currently this is novel. However, within a few years it will just be expected.

Given that all successful future software vendors will have to produce transparent and highly mashable applications, the key factor in determining market dominance will be the position of the price barrier. As illustrated in figure 7.1, this is the imaginary wall – or 'paywall' – that separates a customer from something they want. Suppose, for example, that somebody wants to use a word processor. As shown at the top of the figure, traditionally the price barrier has separated them from the entire application. Several hundred pounds, dollars or yen have therefore had to be paid upfront before the customer could type even a three-line memo. This is also the software model that has made companies like Microsoft fat.

(a) Traditional price barrier prevents any use before payment.

(b) Cloud price barrier allows some free use, with payment only required for support, extensive use or additional services.

Figure 7.1: Repositioning the price barrier

In the bottom half of figure 7.1, we see how the price barrier can be moved in the Age of the Cloud. Here an online word processor like Google Docs, Zoho Writer or Adobe Buzzword may be used without any upfront payment. In fact, there is only a charge to overcome the price barrier if a user seeks support or has extensive usage or additional service requirements. Try before you buy is therefore possible, with nobody paying in advance for unnecessary or unsuitable functionality.

The reason that the price barrier can be moved away from the customer is that basic, free services can now be supplied extremely cheaply online. Way back in chapter one I explained how cloud computing is dynamically scalable and has no fixed costs. Very significantly, this is true not only in consumption but also in supply. The cost of servicing an additional user of Google Docs or Zoho Writer – or what economists call the marginal cost – is so low that it is not worth charging for. However, technical support, large quantities of online storage and the customization of a service to meet the needs of an individual customer cannot be as easily scaled for next-to-nothing. Companies therefore have to charge for services to the right of the price barrier.

Cloud computing vendors need to carefully position the price barrier to maximize the profits they can earn from those customers on its right-hand side. However, they also need to keep it far enough from the left to obtain and maintain a strong market position by offering a free service to those users with minimal service requirements.

In time advertising is likely to be used to generate a revenue stream from users on the left-hand side of the price barrier. Already the 'free' version of Microsoft Office Web Apps is funded by advertising. It is therefore likely that in time more and more of our word processors, spreadsheets and other applications may be paid for by companies trying to sell us stuff.

The infrastructure frontier
For most individuals and businesses, computing infra-structure is going to become just as irrelevant as software. In ten years, hardly any of us will be spending a significant amount of money on hardware boxes, be they PCs or servers in a data centre. Instead, we will access the cloud using relatively cheap, low-power computing devices, with

most of our processing power and storage 'out there' in the cloud. However, somebody will still need to run the cloud computing data centres on which we will rely. A battle is therefore starting to brew on the infrastructure frontier.

All cloud computing vendors directly or indirectly provide us with infrastructure. Infrastructure as a service (IaaS) providers, such as Amazon, GoGrid and Rackspace, directly provide server capacity, as do all platform as a service (PaaS) vendors, including Microsoft Azure and Force.com. Most online software providers also directly deliver online processing power and storage with their applications. However, others piggyback their online applications on the infrastructure of other providers. For example, many companies host their applications on Amazon Web Services, Force.com or Google App Engine. That said, it is unlikely that any company without its own data centres will prove successful in the Battle for the Cloud.

The above means that a very significant investment in infrastructure is becoming essential for success in the computing business. This also represents a critical about turn for the industry. In recent decades software companies, such as Microsoft and Adobe, have become powerful by selling software to run on their customers' hardware. Hardware vendors, such as Apple, Dell and IBM, have also largely generated their profits by selling hardware to customers instead of investing in it themselves and renting it out.

By allowing customers to rent computer power on demand, cloud computing is turning the computing industry into a very capital-intensive business. Indeed, in a sense cloud computing is all about moving the fixed costs of computing infrastructure from customers to online providers.

Another aspect of the infrastructure frontier is environmental leadership. Computing already accounts for about 2 per cent of global carbon dioxide emissions – or roughly the same as aviation. Centralizing infrastructure in the cloud ought to be highly beneficial for the environment. This is because cloud vendors will be able to run their data centres at a far more optimal capacity than most individuals and businesses. However, due to their sheer scale, cloud data centres will also be highly scrutinized by businesses, governments and the green lobby.

Google already has an annual electricity bill of over $300 million. The company therefore invests heavily in the development of more energy-efficient computer power supplies, and was one of the founders of an industry body called the Climate Savers Computing Initiative. IBM also has a $1bn energy-saving project called Big Green. In time, other major cloud vendors will have to be just as proactive in signalling and providing as low-carbon a computing infrastructure as they can.

The access frontier

As explained in the last chapter, computing will increasingly involve the use of devices that are not traditional PCs. Most major cloud computing contenders have therefore already taken at least some kind of stake in the control and development of new access devices.

Control of cloud access devices is being fought over for two reasons. Firstly, access devices provide a means of physically branding the interface to the cloud that lies around in our office, home, car, bag or pocket. Secondly, control of access hardware additionally provides a means of locking in customers to a particular company's applications, infrastructure and content.

Battles on the cloud access frontier may also extend to the Internet service provider (ISP) marketplace. That said, as any telecoms company will lament, providing a connection to the Internet has already become a cut-throat, low-margin business. Early in the Internet revolution, companies such as America Online (AOL) that tried to integrate Internet access and content were also unsuccessful. This said, Google's recent decision to build a fibre-optic network to offer very high-speed broadband in the United States may signal a future trend for cloud vendors to become ISPs.

The content services frontier

At the end of the day, the content that people obtain, manipulate, create and store is what cloud computing is all about. In many respects, the software, infrastructure and access frontiers are therefore no more than a means to an end.

The great danger for all cloud computing companies is that they become the custodians of vast computer warehouses filled with content that is highly valuable but owned by others. In part this is inevitable, as business and personal data will always be third-party property. However, the ownership and supply of most forms of public media and information is still very much up for grabs.

Google not only monopolizes the search business, but is currently trying to become the digital repository of the world's books. Along with Microsoft, Google also has a stranglehold on public, web-based mapping services. Meanwhile, Apple has used iTunes to obtain a very significant slice of the online audio and video download industry. Amazon is currently the most successful supplier of e-books and is also obtaining a strong stake in online music and video. However, none of these positions is unassailable.

There are also many other content and services frontiers up for grabs. These include the hosting of augmented reality worlds, the warehousing of objects digitized for 3D printing, and the creation of online voice and vision recognition systems.

Ultimately, success on the content services frontier will come down to which companies manage to digitize and deliver the most things that human beings actually care about. It is also worth pointing out that, in the longer term, the companies that achieve this may not even be within the current computing, communications or media industries.

Cloud Contenders

Any really strong contender in the Battle for the Cloud needs to fight on all frontiers. This means that standout candidates have to provide access to transparent computing applications and infrastructure, while also demonstrating environmental leadership. They additionally have to control at least some forms of cloud access, as well as some of the content that users find and manipulate when they go online.

Today, the three computing giants that meet the above criteria are Google, Microsoft and Apple. Strong contenders also include Amazon and industry stalwart IBM. Other firms are likely to play a significant role in cloud computing. However, given the infrastructure costs now required to enter the market in a big way, it is the aforementioned five organizations that we most need to watch. The following sections therefore examine how their fortunes are likely to stack up and interrelate.

Google

Google was one of the most successful Dot Com start-ups. Since it was formed in 1998, the company has also rapidly grown to compete strongly on all four cloud computing frontiers. It is therefore now very well placed to dominate the cloud.

Google already has loads of online applications. These include Gmail, Google Docs, Google Calendar, Google Translate, Google Goggles and Google Wave. Google also runs its Google Gadgets web services app store, and in March 2010 launched Google Apps Marketplace. The latter allows other vendors to integrate their applications into the Google Apps business suite that was initially just based around Gmail, Google Calendar and Google Docs. Given that the range of third-party applications available already include accounting, payroll, marketing, project management and training applications, pretty much anything a business wants to do can now be done with Google Apps. There is even a third-party application called Skytap Cloud that enables businesses to run their existing applications in Google Apps so that 'no app is left behind'.

As if the above range of software offerings were not enough, in 2009 Google released its own web browser. The company's Android operating system additionally ships on 60,000 Internet-enabled mobile devices every day. By late 2010, Google will also have launched a new PC operating system.

To make things initially confusing, Google's web browser and PC operating system are both called 'Chrome'. However, read on and you will discover the cool logic behind this apparent madness! The free, downloadable Chrome web browser was written from scratch to be a faster, more stable and more secure means of accessing the web. While Chrome's share of the browser marketplace is currently tiny, there is no doubt that its browser is very fast and the best for accessing online applications. I am in fact writing in Google Docs running in Google Chrome right now!

At least on mobile devices, Google's Chrome OS operating system is a direct competitor to Microsoft Windows. The idea is to merge an operating system with a web browser, which is why the Chrome browser and Chrome OS share the same name. As Google argue, most of the time we turn on our computers, wait for our operating system to load, and then run a web browser. The intention with Chrome OS is simply to cut out the stage of loading the operating system. Computers running Chrome OS will therefore boot very quickly straight to the Internet, with all applications accessed from the cloud.

Unlike Microsoft Windows, Chrome OS is free. However, it is not a conventional operating system that can be downloaded or bought on a disk and installed. As Google explain:

> As a consumer, the way you get Google Chrome OS is by buying a netbook that has Google Chrome OS installed by the manufacturer. Google Chrome OS is being developed to run on new machines that are specially optimized for increased security and performance. We are working with manufacturers to develop reference hardware for Google Chrome OS. These netbooks will be available in the fourth quarter of 2010.

Chrome OS really is the operating system for the Cloud Computing Age. Because it is restricted to specially optimized hardware, Chrome OS not only boots up in less than ten seconds, but is also very secure. Remember how in chapter five I suggested that the best cloud access devices would be virtually non-programmable? Well, a computer running Chrome OS meets this criterion.

As Google puts it, a Chrome OS access device is a 'totally rethought computer that will let you focus on the Internet, so you can stop worrying about your computer'. In fact, Chrome OS does not even need anti-virus software. This is because all software applications run on the Internet and not on the user's computing device. Google also intends to monitor what happens in web applications accessed by Chrome OS to prevent malicious activity.

OK, so I am already nine paragraphs into discussing Google and we have not even got past its software armoury! We should therefore rapidly move on to consider how Google competes on the infrastructure frontier. In this part of the cloud, Google has its App Engine PaaS offering, as well as Google Sites for hosting web pages. Like all Google services, these run on the very many servers that reside in Google's data centres.

Exactly how many data centres Google has is shrouded in secrecy, but most reports suggest the number is between thirty and forty, with space also rented in others. These include nineteen data centres in use or under construction in the US, twelve in Europe, three in Asia, one in Russia and one in South America. Some analysts estimate that, in total, Google's data centres contain over two million servers.

While Google is certainly a very major provider of cloud infrastructure, this is probably the cloud frontier on which the company is weakest. Unlike Amazon, 3Tera, Rackspace, IBM and others, Google does not currently sell infrastructure as a service. Rather, its strategy is to provide infrastructure for its own applications, or for applications that its customers build using Google tools.

On the third Battle for the Cloud frontier of cloud access, Google has also been increasingly busy. Its Android operating system now runs on mobile phones from several manufacturers, as well as being embedded on several models of netbook. In 2010, Google also ventured into hardware with the launch of its very own Nexus One smartphone. At the time of writing, it looks extremely likely that in 2011 Google will launch a tablet running Chrome OS to compete with Apple's iPad. Oh, and as mentioned a few pages back, Google is now building a fibre-optic network to bring really high-speed broadband into the home in the US.

All of the above developments aside, the majority of people still most associate Google with its search engine. So much is this the case that the verb 'to Google' has become part of our language.

Google makes a lot of money by selling advertising on its search engine. In fact, the company handles more than 75 per cent of all search-related advertising in the world. Search is also going to get smarter, with Google now experimenting with voice- and vision-based search via Google Goggles. Point your mobile device at something and Google will upload the picture or video, work out what it is, and return relevant information. Google Translate now also lets us look at any web page in over fifty languages. A related system that will translate our mobile phone calls as we speak is also said to be less than two years away. When it comes to allowing us to find and access content, there are no signs that Google will cease to be the top player in the cloud.

Google is also on a content-gathering spree. YouTube – the video hosting website that plays out over a billion movies a day – is now owned by Google. This includes ownership of YouTube EDU (YouTube.com/edu), which even at launch in March 2009 included around 20,000 videos from over 200 full university courses offered by the likes of MIT, Stanford and Yale. Much of the best educational content in the world is therefore already on a Google server.

Google is also digitizing the world's books. Already it has stored seven million of them in its data centres with the help of 20,000 content partners. Around one million of these books are already available for full preview. This means that if you go to books.google.com you can read the entirety of these books for free.

While Google cannot provide full access to books that are still in copyright or for which it does not have suitable rights, all of the books it has digitized are nevertheless fully searchable. By serving up online 'fair use snippets', Google claims that it is not breaking copyright. Hardly surprisingly, not everybody agrees. However, the day when everything in print will be in the Google database is not that far away. The company does after all already keep track of everything on the web.

In addition to storing most of our words and videos, Google also has maps of every part of the planet, with the Moon and Mars thrown in for good measure. The opportunities to use this incredible database in the development of artificial intelligence are also very significant.

Perhaps Google's smartest strategy is in recognizing that computing access devices can be fairly dumb if the data centres they access are smart. As we will see in chapter ten, artificial intelligences hosted in the cloud are already starting to learn from every user interaction. Google's first highly successful application was a search engine that was taught how to be better by all of us. We should therefore not ignore the fact that Google's online applications and access devices continue to teach Google's systems to become smarter every minute.

Microsoft

While Google looks almost certain to be a major player in the first full decade of cloud computing, many are already writing off Microsoft as the giant of the personal computing era. The relative demise of Bill Gates' corporate baby may indeed be somewhat likely. However, we should not discount Microsoft just yet.

As argued by *The Economist* in October 2009, although thousands of companies offer cloud services, Google, Microsoft and Apple play in a completely different league. All three are engaged in battle on all four cloud computing frontiers. However, based on their financial years ending in

2009, Microsoft has the largest turnover at $58.4bn, with Apple at $34.6bn and Google at $22.3bn. In financial terms Microsoft is therefore almost as large as both of its main competitors put together.

Microsoft's problem is that embracing the cloud means throwing away the core business model that made it a success. There are also very few examples of companies that have ever succeeded in such a move. Looking back to the history of the computing industry, IBM dominated computing's third generation with its System 360 mainframe. The company was also clearly convinced that it could dominate the fourth age of computing by selling PCs to its own open standard. However, what actually happened was that the industry and its customers said 'thank you for the standard', and purchased their PCs from other suppliers. They did not, as IBM had hoped, remain loyal to IBM as the biggest-brand hardware manufacturer. Quite possibly, Microsoft is making a similar mistake right now by banking on our brand loyalty to the last-generation market leader. Though what else can Microsoft do?

Microsoft seems to be assuming that we will always use its software because for two decades most of us have. However, we should all remember that twenty years ago most people ran software from other manufacturers. As anybody over forty knows, WordPerfect and Lotus were for many years the dominant suppliers of word processing and spreadsheet software.

Today many people find it hard to imagine a computer industry not dominated by Microsoft. However, computing has always been led by those companies that have delivered the most customer value at a particular point in time. Just as Microsoft displaced IBM as the dominant force in personal computing when software became more valuable than hardware, so we should not be surprised if Google and others displace Microsoft as software ceases to be what creates most user value.

While it may have been slow to embrace the cloud, Microsoft is nevertheless becoming a cloud computing convert. In a speech in March 2010, Microsoft CEO Steve Ballmer even claimed to be 'betting the company' on cloud computing. In part he argued this to be on the basis that 'the cloud fuels Microsoft, and Microsoft fuels the cloud'. Concurrent with this speech, Microsoft happened to launch a new cloud services website at microsoft.com/cloud.

The reason for Microsoft's apparent change of heart is not too hard to fathom. For example, according to a study by IDC in September 2009, 20 per cent of companies are already using Google Docs widely in their workplace. This is clearly something that Microsoft cannot ignore. In the summer of 2010, its response was to launch the Office Web Apps versions of Word, Excel and PowerPoint as one element of Office 2010. As Microsoft explain:

> Office Web Apps extend the Microsoft Office programs you already know – Word, PowerPoint, Excel and OneNote – with the added benefits of anywhere-access and easy sharing. When you click on an Office document that is stored [online] . . . the document opens directly in your browser. The document looks the same in the browser as it does in the Office program, and Office Web Apps also allow you to edit documents in the browser, using the familiar look and feel of Office. When you want to make changes beyond what is available in the browser, you can easily open the document in an Office program on your computer, and then save it back to the document library.

As the above signals, the explicit intention of Office Web Apps is to complement and not to replace traditional, locally installed software. In turn this suggests that Microsoft's strategy for the cloud is not entirely consistent. On the application frontier, the company still seems to be banking on us all continuing to purchase and install local software, with Office Web Apps merely an addition to a local version of Office. However, on the cloud infrastructure frontier, in 2009 Microsoft opened two new data centres accommodating around half a million servers. It also combined its Windows Azure group with its Windows Server & Solutions group to create a new organization called the Microsoft Server & Cloud Division.

The best explanation for Microsoft's apparent schizophrenia is that it expects office software to remain largely local, while business applications will increasingly be delivered from the cloud. Unfortunately, this flies in the face of all current cloud computing trends, with office and creative applications already moving into the cloud well ahead of most dedicated business systems. Of course it may simply be that Microsoft is happy to sell its new Azure platform into the cloud infrastructure marketplace, while not accepting that its local office applications business is about to be radically transformed.

Microsoft remains a very successful organization with a marketing machine that still skilfully manages to tell many people and companies how to think. It is also competing on all four cloud computing frontiers. For example, Microsoft continues to be involved in creating new access devices. These currently include the development of the Microsoft Surface table-size surface computer mentioned in the last chapter. Microsoft is also developing Windows 7 tablet or 'slate' computers with partners including HP and Archos.

Furthermore, Microsoft is continuing to develop its Windows Mobile operating system under the snappy new name of 'Windows Phone 7 Series'. This is used on

Internet-enabled mobile phones from many manufacturers. However, Windows Phone 7 Series faces very stiff competition from phones running Google's Android operating system and Apple's already iconic iPhone.

Lastly on the content services frontier, in 2009 Microsoft yet again relaunched its search engine. Following its previous thrilling names of 'Live Search', 'Windows Live Search' and 'MSN Search', this now bears the exciting label 'Bing'. Today Bing is the third largest search engine on the web, if still dwarfed by Google throughout most of the world and by Baidu in China. However, Bing does go head-to-head very well with Google when it comes to providing online maps.

Apple

A competitor to Microsoft from its earliest days, Apple is perhaps best described as an increasingly successful maverick. The brainchild of Steve Wozniak and former hacker Steve Jobs, the company was formed in 1976, only a year after Bill Gates quit his studies at Harvard to start Microsoft.

Apple launched its iconic Apple I and Apple II personal computers in the 1970s and 1980s. From the very beginning, Apple has also managed to cultivate and maintain an almost fanatical customer base. The cult that surrounds Apple's hardware, software and online content services may also prove to be a key trump card in the Battle for the Cloud.

Compared with Google and Microsoft, Apple is a more straightforward company to analyse. This is because it has pretty much always maintained control of the hardware and software components of a restricted range of products. Indeed, only briefly in the 1990s did Apple ever allow other manufacturers to make computers capable of running Apple software.

Like Microsoft, Apple is at present rather conservative on the software frontier. The company offers two cloud services – MobileMe and iWork.com – that both complement, rather than replace, locally installed software. MobileMe is an online e-mail, contacts and calendar service used to synchronize the information on different Apple devices, such as an Apple Mac and an iPhone. The service also includes Gallery for creating online photo albums, as well as iDisk for storing and sharing files online. After a sixty-day free trial, MobileMe costs $99 a year. In comparison to competitor offerings, this is somewhat expensive.

iWork.com integrates with Apple's iWork office software to allow people to share their files online. Like Microsoft Office Web Apps, iWork.com is therefore an additional feature within a traditional, locally installed software package. iWork.com does allow documents, spreadsheets and presentations to be shared in the cloud and accessed on any device via a web browser. However, without iWorks installed, shared files can only be viewed, not edited.

While Apple does not currently sell cloud platform or infrastructure services, in 2009 the company started to build a new, 500,000-square-foot data centre in North Carolina. Whether this billion-dollar investment is intended to support the delivery of existing cloud services or to facilitate the launch of major new offerings is yet to be announced. However, any investment of this magnitude by a major cloud computing contender cannot be ignored.

On the access frontier, Apple is already a very strong contender with its successful range of desktop and notebook computers, coupled with its iPhone and iPad. As processing power and data migrate into the cloud, mobile devices that are secure and reliable are going to be in increasing demand. The loyalty that Apple continues to instil in its customers to continue to buy its mobile computing devices may therefore become increasingly significant.

On the final frontier of cloud content and services, Apple is nicely positioned with its iTunes Store. This is already the source of most media downloaded to Apple iPhones, iPads and iPod media players. Millions of non-Apple converts have also installed iTunes on their computers to allow them to purchase content from the store. So popular is iTunes that in February 2010 it delivered its ten billionth download.

iTunes is also very significant as the world's biggest app store. This part of iTunes already offers over 140,000 applications that can be downloaded to an iPhone or iPad. The vast majority of these applications have not been created by Apple. However, ownership of the iTunes App Store still allows Apple control of the content that ends up on Apple hardware.

Within the iTunes store, Apple has also established a dedicated educational area called iTunes U. This is a competitor to Google's YouTube EDU, and features video and audio content from colleges and universities including Stanford, UC Berkeley, Duke and MIT. Concurrently with the launch of its iPad, Apple also announced a new online bookshop called Apple iBooks.

Amazon

An often forgotten but highly significant contender in the Battle for the Cloud is Amazon. Like Google, Amazon is a very successful child of the Dot Com boom. The company does not currently offer cloud computing applications, but is a very strong contender when it comes to cloud infrastructure. With its Kindle e-book reader, the sale of e-books and downloadable music, and Amazon Video on Demand, the company also has significant stakes on the access and content services cloud computing frontiers.

As explained in chapter four, Amazon offers a suite of cloud hosting products under the banner of Amazon Web Services (AWS). These include Elastic Compute Cloud (EC2) and the Simple Storage Service (S3). Both are now being used by a very wide range of private and public sector organizations to run applications and store data in the cloud. Amazon has already formed partnerships or made other arrangements with IBM, Microsoft and Oracle to allow traditional software from these companies to run on virtual servers housed in Amazon data centres. None of this activity is very public or widely reported. However, it does place Amazon in a strong position as the computing company to which many businesses will turn when they decide to migrate their business systems online.

When it comes to cloud access, Amazon has to date focused exclusively on the development and sale of its Kindle e-book readers. These are now the best-selling products on Amazon.com and the most popular e-book readers in the world. Books are downloaded to a Kindle wirelessly, with over 420,000 titles now available. By controlling the access device, Amazon is already gaining some level of monopoly in the supply of e-books themselves. Amazon's battle with Apple's iPad and iBooks store will be an interesting one to watch.

Amazon has also waded into the more traditional media download market. Its music download service Amazon MP3 launched in May 2007, followed by Amazon Video on Demand the following September. This puts Amazon in competition with Apple's iTunes on all fronts, although its video download service is currently only available in the US.

IBM

International Business Machines is the grandfather of the computing industry. The company's roots date back to the merger of the Tabulating Machine Company, the International Time Recording Company and the Computing Scale Company of America in 1911. IBM has been building electronic computational devices since the 1950s. The fact that it is still in business when so many of its early competitors have fallen has to mean that it knows a thing or two about delivering what businesses want.

In 2009 IBM entered the Battle for the Cloud in a fairly big way. On the applications frontier it launched a range of cloud-collaboration tools under the banner 'LotusLive'. These include LotusLive iNotes, which provides web-based e-mail and calendar functions, together with the LotusLive Connections business social networking suite. These enterprise social networking tools are also something that competitors, such as Google, currently lack.

In October 2009 IBM announced that it was getting into the cloud data storage business with its Smart Business Storage Cloud service. This is a private cloud offering that competes with the Simple Storage Service (S3) part of Amazon Web Services. IBM is, however, somewhat dismissive of Amazon and its other competitors, which it claims offer cloud services that are unsuitable for 'mission-critical or enterprise grade' applications. This is, of course, just the view from IBM! However, as with Apple in the mobile access device marketplace, brand and customer confidence still matter a great deal. In February 2010 IBM signed a contract with the US Airforce to design a secure, private cloud computing infrastructure capable of supporting nearly 100 bases and 700,000 active military personnel. At present, it is unlikely that any other cloud computing vendor would have been seriously considered for such a contract.

Data Centres, App Stores and Mobile Devices

As IBM's US Airforce contract indicates, cloud computing is becoming a very big and very serious business. All contenders in the Battle for the Cloud therefore potentially have a very great deal to lose and to gain. Critically, all major players need to continue to invest heavily in data centres and the servers that they house. In turn this will make mistakes expensive. Remember that one of the greatest benefits of cloud computing for its users is that it shifts fixed infrastructure investment costs from the customer to the supplier.

Over the next few years, probably the most significant and interesting skirmishes will be those between Apple with its iPhone and iPad, Google with Android and Chrome OS, and possibly Microsoft with Windows Phone 7 Series. Any company that manages to reign supreme on this mobile access device frontier is likely to maintain control of the app store from which most of us will obtain our mobile device applications. Such applications will, in turn, also increasingly depend on cloud data supplied by the company that controls the access device. The battle for mobile device and mobile device operating system dominance will therefore be fierce as it will determine not just which device we use, but also which app store we download from, and the music, videos, e-books and augmented realities we daily consume.

We should also be aware that the dominant mobile device operating system is very likely to migrate to the desktop. There is already no technical reason why a desktop or traditional laptop computer could not run Apple's iPhone/iPad OS and applications, or Google Chrome, Google Android or even Windows Phone 7 Series. Google Chrome OS and the iPhone/iPad OS may be written for netbooks and tablets. However, the hardware specification of such devices is not that different from current desktop computers, let alone those of tomorrow.

Once we get used to cloud computing, the demand will skyrocket for no-hassle and very secure cloud access devices that boot up extremely quickly. No traditional, installed-application operating system – be it from Microsoft or Apple – is ever likely to be able to offer this. I would therefore predict that we will see desktop, laptop and nettop computers running Chrome OS and iPad/iPhone OS sooner rather than later. The fact that there are already over 140,000 iPad/iPhone applications in the iTunes App Store suddenly becomes very significant indeed. So too does the fact that Chrome OS features a direct link to Google Docs.

* * *

Coming Full Circle?

Gartner has estimated that in 2009 the market for cloud computing services was worth $56.3 billion. It also estimates that cloud computing revenues will grow to $150.1 billion by 2013. This means that there could be several winners in the Battle for the Cloud. A lot of small computing vendors also have the chance to become relatively very successful. However, such small vendors are likely – like the rest of us – to depend on cloud infrastructure provided by a very few large companies.

As we have seen, some of those businesses seeking to dominate the cloud are new players already accustomed to darting nimbly among the dinosaurs. Others are well-established traditional computing companies with legacy brands and business models to match. Inevitably, therefore, motives and strategies towards the cloud are likely to be somewhat varied as the computing industry enters another period of massive shakeout and change.

Ultimately, the Battle for the Cloud will be won by those computing businesses that respond most effectively to two key transitions. The first is the evolution of computers from being devices on which we run programs to devices used to access the Internet. The second is the evolution of business applications and information from being things kept in a data centre to online resources used to run a company. Looked at in this context, Google and Apple are clearly best placed to dominate our use of computers, while Amazon, IBM and Google are currently ahead when it comes to allowing organizations to run their business online.

For companies not in the computing business, the transition to the cloud will lead to a reliance on one or more vendors from whom they will rent services instead of buying hardware and software outright. This is how computing always used to be, and how IBM and others built their pre-personal computing empires. As we will explore in the next chapter, such a new and old state of the world may not be to everybody's liking. However, whoever wins the Battle for the Cloud, cloud computing is still going to be the future.

8

TROUBLE IN THE BOARDROOM

You want to do what?! Are you crazy? No, absolutely not. You just don't understand! And even if you were right there would be far too many risks. I'd personally recommend spending ten times the money on a new server farm. Oh, and maybe a dozen more IT staff. Goodbye!

The above, or something like it, is the likely reaction of many information technology (IT) professionals to any request to try cloud computing. I know. I've been there. And if you are an IT professional and would not say the above, then award yourself a shiny gold star with extra glitter.

With most of the mills closed down, there's very little trouble there. There is, however, trouble brewing in many a boardroom as the potential of cloud computing comes to the attention of more managers who do not work in the IT department. It is also the kind of storm that we have witnessed before.

Back in the 1980s and 1990s, many IT departments were highly resistant to the use of PCs for 'serious' computing. Even when desktop machines became fairly commonplace, personal computing developments continued to be strongly resisted by many IT staff. For example, I remember being told by a large IT department that Microsoft Windows would never be rolled-out because 'it was not stable and would never catch on'. Well, they were at least half right about that one.

Purchasing More Paper Cutters

In 1993, IT guru Dan Trimmer wrote a book called *Downsizing: Strategies for Success in the Modern Computer World*. This influential tome was all about the replacement of mainframe computers with 'downsized' systems based on networks of PCs. Most of the chapters in Trimmer's book emphasized the need to convince traditionalists of the rising power of the personal computer. Indeed, perhaps the most significant message was that those who needed enlightening the most were often a company's IT professionals.

Today's transition from internal IT resources to at least some uptake of cloud computing mirrors exactly the downsizing shift from mainframes to PCs twenty years ago. Like downsizing, cloud computing represents a radical transition that challenges the status quo and threatens the careers of IT staff. It is for this reason that some managers may have learnt things from this book that their IT department really ought to have told them already.

For years it has been recognized that a 'disconnect' frequently exists between a business and its IT department. In 1994, Charles Wang – the Chief Executive of IT giant Computer Associates – documented this rift in a great book called *Techno Vision*. Like Dan Trimmer a year earlier, Wang noted how it was often non-IT employees who first saw the value of new IT developments, such as personal computing. He also observed how IT department staff then often tried to prevent the exploitation of such developments. In turn, this frequently fuelled the division between IT and the rest of the business, making things even worse.

Techno Vision recounts the tale of a journalist who, in the late 1980s, interviewed the IT manager of a very large company. One of the things she asked was how many PCs the company had. The answer she rapidly obtained was 267, which even at the time seemed rather low. However, two days later the journalist received a phone call to say that the company actually had at least 1,100 PCs and was still counting!

The reason the IT manager had not known how many PCs their company had was both alarming and very simple. Across the business, employees knew that the IT department disapproved of PCs and hampered their purchase. To avoid such hassle, most users therefore bought PCs as 'office equipment', with their purchase orders listing their new hardware as 'calculators', 'typewriters', 'desk accessories' and even 'paper cutters'.

The above story was representative of much common practice in the late 1980s and early 1990s. At the time, a great many PCs crept into companies under the noses of their IT departments. This was simply because covert purchasing provided the easiest route to experiment with and deploy early spreadsheets and other new-fangled desktop applications. As I hope you appreciate, the reason for recounting this here is that exactly the same thing is already starting to happen today with cloud computing.

Twenty years ago, non-IT people were increasingly saying 'we don't need the IT department and its data centre, we can just have our own PC'. Today, people are similarly starting to say 'we don't need the IT department and its data centre, we can just cloud compute'. Neither statement was, or is, entirely sensible or an appropriate state of affairs. However, the parallel is striking and cannot be ignored.

Business computing is changing dramatically once again. As I hope the other chapters in this book have demonstrated, cloud computing is no longer a crazy idea but a solid reality. Today a great many people within companies are starting to cloud compute regardless of the protestations of many of their IT departments. Once users have an Internet connection, they can simply log on to Google Docs, Zoho or whatever cloud offering they wish and just get on with it.

Over the past few years, some people have informed me that covert cloud computing will not happen in their organization because their IT department blocks access to certain websites. Particularly in the public sector, this is often the case. However, netbooks, laptops, smartphones and tablets increasingly have a wireless 3G Internet connection that is beyond IT department control. Most managers – and collaborative groups thereof – can therefore now try cloud computing if they really want to. The issue is simply whether or not they have to purchase a new, wireless device to access the cloud, and if so whether they have to list it on their purchase order as a 'paper cutter'. Of course it would be far better if this never had to happen. Whatever else, smart IT departments now ought at the very least to be offering those users who want it a means of accessing cloud computing resources in a secure and well-managed fashion.

Embracing the Cloud

Cloud computing should not arrive in any business with only the narrowest, gritted-teeth support of its IT department. Not least this is due to cloud computing's medium-term inevitability. IT departments and IT professionals now rapidly have to decide whether they want to be part of the cloud computing steamroller or the traditional computing road.

Back in chapter one I outlined how cloud computing will become the only show in town for three reasons. These were that cloud computing will be essential to remain competitive, to be green, and to develop and run next-generation applications. At present, most early adopters of cloud computing have made their leap of faith due to a desire to become more competitive by reducing their IT costs. This is also hardly surprising given that vendors like Force.com have now published audited figures that indicate how their customers can develop new applications at half their traditional cost. However, the rewards for cloud computing adoption are already exceeding bottom-line IT cost savings.

In December 2009, a report by KPMG in Australia highlighted how early adopters of cloud computing are not only reducing their IT costs, but gaining broader business efficiency benefits. These benefits were stemming from their ability to very rapidly scale computing resources according to the needs of the business, as well as the adoption of utility-based pricing. This is all very good news. However, the same report also noted that many IT managers still considered cloud computing 'immature' and no more than an 'interesting concept' rather than a strategic necessity.

It is also not only some internal IT departments that are having to be dragged kicking and screaming into the Cloud Computing Age. The last chapter may have detailed the Battle for the Cloud now being fought out in the computing industry. However, it also needs to be acknowledged that many current computing providers have made no move whatsoever to embrace the cloud.

As noted in a speech by BT's chief scientist J. P. Rangaswami in February 2010, the opportunity that cloud computing offers to 'compress' wasted internal hardware and software resources is still very much being 'pushed back' by suppliers. As he further argued, 'Who stands to lose if the way we license software changes dramatically? People don't like talking about the fact that there's a $200bn industry that's desperate not to become a $50bn industry.'

There can be no getting away from the fact that when a company adopts cloud computing, it will need to purchase fewer internal IT resources. It will also require fewer people to maintain them. Most companies will still need some internal IT staff to service their internal networks and Internet connectivity, to develop and maintain their applications, and to install and service their cloud access devices and peripherals. Many larger firms are also likely to maintain a small data centre in the same way that they kept some mainframes after the PC revolution. There are also going to be new jobs created within cloud computing vendors. This all said, those IT departments, IT staff and IT suppliers who are not smart enough to become part of the steamroller rather than part of the road have very little incentive to support let alone promote cloud computing. In turn, this will place many non-IT-literate managers in the difficult position of trying to advance a cloud computing strategy without the support of those technical experts on whom they have come to rely. Any manager interviewing a new member of IT staff is therefore advised to ask them about their perspective on cloud computing.

Advancing the Business Case

Unless they are prepared to forgo substantial business benefits, most managers will have to at least partially wean their companies off old computing practices. This is also exactly what their predecessors had to do during the PC revolution. Cloud computing is no more of a panacea than personal computing was twenty years ago. However, some of its benefits are now pretty much undeniable and ought not to be ignored regardless of the protestations of many IT professionals and suppliers.

In most organizations, managers are likely to advance cloud computing via a straightforward business case. At least initially, this is likely to identify how cloud computing can be used to help a company do very routine computing tasks more efficiently, as well as to accomplish entirely new things.

As Nicholas Carr points out in his cloud computing manifesto *The Big Switch*, it is an inescapable fact that the server computers in most companies typically run at about 20 to 30 per cent capacity. In contrast, most cloud data centres are able to run their servers at around 80 per cent utilization. This enables cloud computing vendors to reap significant cost and environmental savings that they can, in part, pass on to their customers while still making a profit. Any business therefore needs a very good reason not to move at least some of its more routine applications and data storage into the cloud.

At the other end of the spectrum, few organizations will be able to ignore the opportunities for collaborative working and application innovation made possible by cloud computing. Most companies will also not want to risk being invisible when their customers gaze at the world through augmented reality browsers. In the last decade most companies had to venture on to the web. This decade, most businesses will similarly need to at least partially embrace the cloud if they want to remain competitive.

All this implies that the most basic and most innovative aspects of business computing will rapidly migrate into the cloud. Due to cost savings and collaborative opportunities, it will be very difficult for anybody to argue for bread-and-butter computing activities such as e-mail, office applications and end-user file storage to remain in-house. Supporting these kinds of activities may be what many IT departments currently spend at least half of their time on. However, it is unlikely that they will be able to continue to provide this kind of support in a manner that will make competitive sense. Cloud vendors including Google, Zoho and Adobe already offer improved service levels at a lower cost. For example, a transition to Google Apps typically provides a company's employees with fifty times more e-mail filestore (25Gb) than the industry average, while at the same time saving the business money.

At the new applications end of the IT spectrum, most collaborative applications and new forms of web service are a no-brainer to build and host in the cloud. In most companies, what will therefore be fought over will be the fate of those in-house computer systems that are neither highly generic nor highly innovative and naturally cloud-centric. Such 'computing-in-the-middle' systems typically include those used to administer production, sales, marketing, stock-control and accounting. Whether and when they will move into the cloud is also likely to depend on a company's level of strategic foresight.

The Fate of Computing-in-the-Middle

From the perspective of anybody looking outwards from today, most computing-in-the-middle is likely to appear just fine as it is. Some of it will migrate to the cloud when it needs to be upgraded or requires collaborative functionality. However, most IT departments will be pretty loath to let it go. Indeed, there is already some anecdotal evidence that IT managers are accepting a move to cloud e-mail and office applications in return for an assurance that most dedicated business systems will not leave their data centres.

The above is all well and good until others in the board-room strategically remove themselves from the present and try to imagine where they want their business to be in ten years' time. Once such a foresight perspective is adopted, it is also very difficult not to be won over by the arguments of those like Nicholas Carr who place the transition to cloud computing in a broader historical context.

Carr's contention is that the shift from in-house to cloud computing today mirrors exactly the transition from in-house to external power generation a century ago. In the early 1900s, most companies had made the transition from wind, water or steam to electric power. However, they still generated their own electricity themselves. Given that throughout the Industrial Revolution practically all companies had been responsible for making their own power, the idea of plugging in to a public power grid was simply unthinkable. Electricity had become the lifeblood of most factories. Relying on another business for its supply was therefore initially viewed as far too great a risk.

As we are all aware, it is now exceedingly rare for a business to generate its own electricity. Relatively few organizations even have their own back-up generators. Alongside cost and efficiency savings, what was needed to embrace the switch to public electricity generation a century ago was therefore a mindset shift. The same thing also applies today when it comes to moving computing-in-the-middle into the cloud.

In 1900 virtually every company generated its own power. However, by 1930 almost all obtained electricity from a public grid. With this powerful parallel in mind, managers with strategic foresight today are likely to conclude that in a decade or so very few companies will have much internal IT. The only difference between the past and present 'big switch' is that computing will become a mainstream utility service far more rapidly than electricity did a century ago.

The rate of advancement in computer hardware development currently shows no sign of slowing down. As a consequence, whether or not they plan to embrace the cloud, very few companies will be running their existing computing infrastructure in five years' time. Legacy investment will therefore prove only a minor impediment to slow the eventual industrial transition to cloud computing.

Moving computing-in-the-middle to the cloud will not mean that IT departments will cease to exist. Nor will it mean that IT departments will lose control of a company's computing applications. However, moving computing-in-the-middle to the cloud will mean that the IT department will write and maintain applications that run elsewhere on somebody else's infrastructure. This will also save the business money, transfer all fixed investment costs to cloud vendors, increase flexibility and employee collaboration, enable new types of application, and make environmental compliance in the data centre somebody else's problem.

Balancing Hybrid Solutions

While cloud computing offers strong strategic merits in the long term, I must again stress that at present it is neither a panacea nor in all cases an instant fix. Even for the most foresight-rich organizations, business-wide cloud-based computing solutions are unlikely to be sensible or even implementable in the short term. Granted, new business start-ups now have the significant advantage of cloud computing from day one. However, at least for a few years, the best strategy for an existing business will be to implement a transitional or 'hybrid' solution. In other words, for some time to come most companies will have to be selective about what they do and do not do in the cloud.

Several managers have told me that their business will embrace cloud computing gradually and in line with existing plans for server replacement. Such a strategy is also entirely sensible. If a current data centre works there can be little incentive to try and fix it. Gartner estimate that it will take until 2012 before even 20 per cent of businesses have no IT infrastructure. This is precisely because many companies will shift to the cloud only when their existing hardware needs replacing.

Even in the long term, cloud computing does not have to be an all-or-nothing strategy. Just as PCs now happily co-exist with mainframes, so for many years cloud and local systems will function side by side. This means that many businesses are likely to adopt a cloud-as-a-supplement rather than a cloud-as-a-replacement model. Such a hybrid approach must focus on obtaining the right balance of cloud versus local computing. This means that it must allow a business to obtain the greatest benefits from cloud computing, while suffering the fewest actual or potential drawbacks.

The cloud computing drawbacks that companies may wish to avoid include the disruption of successful existing systems, the scrapping of technology that is still being paid for, and exposure to high levels of risk. Companies that rely on off-the-shelf local applications not yet available from the cloud will also be forced to adopt hybrid solutions until there are further developments in the online software marketplace.

Rather than adopting a 'cloud as replacement' or 'cloud as supplement' strategy, a third option that some firms may opt for is known as an 'internal cloud'. This is where a business builds its own cloud computing infrastructure to allow it to internally deliver browser-based software and hardware from its own data centre.

Internal clouds should not to be confused with vendor managed private clouds as discussed in chapter four on page 94. The key difference is that private clouds involve a computing supplier like IBM providing and managing a dedicated cloud infrastructure, while internal clouds do not involve the use of any external vendor infrastructure or expertise. While internal clouds may facilitate employee collaboration and some cost savings, they are not really a true form of cloud computing. Rather, many already view an internal cloud strategy as a last-ditch attempt by an IT department to hold on to its servers and to avoid radical change.

The Cloud Adoption Curve

Cloud computing is now seriously and rapidly entering the mainstream. In the summer of 2009 scepticism was still rife, but by the spring 2010 there was a strong and growing awareness of cloud computing's competitive, environmental and innovatory paybacks. Suggesting that mainstream business computing will remain in-house is like arguing that the horse and cart had any real chance against the internal combustion engine, or that metal type can compete with desktop publishing. As network computing giant Sun Microsystems argued in one of its recent white papers, 'cloud computing is the next generation' and is now well and truly 'taking the information technology world by storm'.

Most analysts are treating 2010 as the first really big year of cloud computing. It is also now widely argued that the transition to mainstream cloud computing will take about a decade. Given such an analysis, figure 8.1 illustrates a likely cloud computing adoption curve.

The vertical axis in figure 8.1 plots the number of firms transitioning in whole or part to cloud computing in a particular year. As the figure shows, between 2005 and 2010 the steadily rising number of firms embracing the cloud were all pioneers. Such companies included the first two million businesses to sign up to Google Apps, those who built the first 400,000 Zoho Creator databases, the initial 70,000 customers of SalesForce.com, the first 15,000 companies to administer their personnel using Employease.com, and the first few thousand businesses to host data and applications on Amazon Web Services.

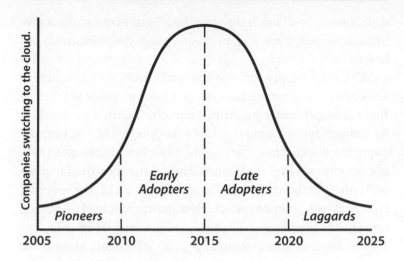

Figure 8.1: The cloud computing adoption curve

Cloud computing's second phase of mainstream early adoption runs from 2010 to 2015. The number of companies involved is expected to peak around 2015, with the second part of the decade comprising a mainstream phase of late adoption. By 2020 it is then likely that we will witness a 'laggard' period in which most of the remaining ostriches will finally get their heads out of the sand and catch up with the rest of us.

All this is, of course, no more than a best guess. However, figure 8.1 ought to get companies and their IT departments thinking about where they want to be on the cloud computing adoption curve. In ten years' time, most companies are likely to be purchasing IT services from the cloud for just the same reason that they will still be purchasing electricity from a national grid. Both IT supply and electricity generation will be things that an external vendor will be able to accomplish far more cost effectively than an in-house department. It will therefore not be to any firm's competitive benefit to purchase and manage computing resources in-house.

While the supply – if not the application – of computing resources will in future cease to give a competitive advantage, there is at present a medium-term competitive payback to be gained from being an early adopter. This is because companies who are early adopters of cloud computing will obtain cost savings and innovation gains that the laggards will not yet be reaping. Granted, by 2020 the playing field will have evened out and few companies will be paying too much for their computing resources. However, the opportunity to run computing more effectively than some competitors for even a few years is something that no sensible business ought to ignore.

A Cloud Computing Action Plan

Every business needs a cloud computing action plan. It may be possible to carry on regardless, like those in the 1990s who thought that having a website was a mere fad. However, companies that choose such a Luddite strategy will have to watch their competitors benefiting from lower costs, new ways of collaborating, lower green taxes, major customer service innovations and smarter IT.

Arguing that every organization needs a cloud computing action plan is not the same as arguing that every organization ought in whole, or part, to switch to cloud computing right now. Let me repeat, cloud computing is not a panacea. In many cases even a cloud-as-a-supplement strategy will take time to implement. However, some kind of action plan should still be in place. Not least this is because some of the customers and suppliers of most businesses will be using collaborative cloud computing tools with which they will expect everybody else to be familiar. For example, given that two million businesses are already using Google Apps and 20 per cent of companies are making at least some use of Google Docs, how long can it be before every business is asked to collaborate on a shared Google document?

Every cloud computing action plan needs to be drawn up to meet the specific requirements of a particular business. However, for companies starting out from scratch, the first five elements ought probably to look something like this:

- Foster champions and encourage experimentation
- Choose a collaborative suite
- Draft a company-wide cloud computing policy
- Implement killer quick-wins
- Develop a broader strategy

Foster champions and encourage experimentation

At least some people in every business need to become familiar with cloud computing. One way to achieve this could be to distribute a great many copies of this book! But OK, such hopeful self-publicity aside, what every business needs to do is to foster some cloud computing champions and to encourage them to experiment.

In the early 1990s, it was not unknown for enlightened companies to set up a few stand-alone PCs that their staff could experiment with to improve their computing familiarity. Today, opportunities similarly need to be made available for enthusiasts to investigate and understand cloud computing. Allowing even one person a few hours a week to experiment with the applications detailed in chapter three may significantly increase an organization's cloud computing knowledge base. It will also motivate that individual to educate others – perhaps via lunchtime workshops – and to start wider experiments. Such experiments do also not have to start within the IT department. They simply have to

involve one or more people who have an interest in getting
their work done more effectively.

For example, the next time a team needs to run a project
or write a report, suggest that they write collaboratively in
Google Docs. Or set up a Zoho Wiki. Or hold some of their
meetings using Adobe ConnectNow. All of these can be set
up for free in just a few minutes. However, they also all need
to be used in a real, live business situation to make people
truly aware of their potential.

Choose a collaborative suite

Soon after experimentation has begun, a business will need
to decide which collaborative suite it is going to adopt across
the company. Google Docs, Zoho, Acrobat.com and all of
the other collaborative office applications now available are
all very flexible. They also share document exchange formats
and can to a large extent be intermixed. However, it remains
helpful for everybody working for a business to adopt the
same system. Each suite has its own benefits and drawbacks.
The key thing is not which a business chooses, but that a
choice is sensibly made and adhered to.

Draft a company-wide cloud computing policy

Once a core collaborative suite is chosen, it is possible for a
business to start writing and communicating at least a one-
page or one-screen cloud computing policy. As explained in
chapter five, in addition to choosing which applications it
will use, every business needs to decide what kinds of data it
is and is not prepared to trust to the cloud.

A cloud computing policy additionally needs to outline
an effective security regime, as previously discussed in
chapter five. This must detail effective password management, the anti-virus and firewall software that needs to be
installed on every cloud access device, and what kinds of

cloud access hardware may be used. By now it should be obvious that by this stage a company's IT department really ought to be involved. Ideally, the IT department should have initiated the drafting of the cloud computing policy. However, I have yet to talk to a significant number of IT managers who have taken this step.

Implement killer quick-wins

Cloud computing will take hold most easily when its champions manage to demonstrate immediate value added. This means that good cloud computing action plans have to involve the identification and implementation of killer 'quick-wins' that will deliver immediate benefits to the business.

Killer quick-wins should also not be hard to find. More effective collaborative working may well be one. For others, the ability to share files too large to send as e-mail attachments can prove a massive killer quick-win. I now regularly share publishing and video files that are tens or hundreds of megabytes in size using my free Google Docs filespace. Usually I do this by uploading such media to a new folder that I then share publicly for a few hours. This means that I can e-mail a link to somebody who does not even have a Google account and they can simply download the file or files they need. This saves me from writing and posting a CD or DVD. It also absolutely staggers most recipients.

Other quick-wins include embedding a chart in a website that is linked to a Google Docs or Zoho spreadsheet, and which will update in real-time. Using the language translate feature in Google Docs is another obvious benefit, as is adopting Google Sites or Zoho Wiki to create a secure company forum within minutes. Just look back to chapter three and get your thinking cap on.

Cloud computing champions may also develop highly specific quick-win applications. For example, I remember a vet who moaned how his colleagues just 'handed out drugs' from the back of the Land Rover and 'only ever billed for half of them'. His solution was to use Zoho Invoice to set up an online invoicing and PayPal payment system. His colleagues were then able to access this online application on a smartphone in a muddy field each time they issued medicine. By introducing this killer quick-win in his practice, this particular vet anticipated savings of around £50,000 a year.

Another killer quick-win was created by a manager in a very large logistics business that ran several warehouses. The problem she identified was that each week some warehouses bought in temporary staff to cope with their anticipated workload, while staff in other nearby warehouses sat idle. Her solution was to create a Google Docs spreadsheet shared between warehouse managers, and in which each could enter their staff available or required for the next week. This spreadsheet was embedded in a private Google Sites website that contained related information, including a Google map showing warehouse locations. The whole thing was created in hours and presented to the board of the manager's company as an example of what could be achieved with simple cloud computing tools, if not apparently by their existing IT department. Once again, the anticipated savings ran into tens of thousands of pounds.

Develop a broader strategy

The previous four stages of a cloud action plan are all about getting the ball rolling. They are also likely to involve no more than the use of basic online software applications, often obtained free or at a minimal cost. However, once the value of cloud computing has been demonstrated and mindsets have started to change, it is time for more fundamental action.

It is at this point that the cloud computing action plans of different businesses have to diverge. However, as this chapter has detailed, each is likely to involve the migration of e-mail and office applications into the cloud, followed by the identification and exploitation of innovative cloud computing opportunities. Next will come the even harder decisions regarding the potential transfer of computing-in-the-middle core business applications to PaaS or IaaS vendors. Almost inevitably, this will be where battles with the IT department are likely to spill into the boardroom. Revolution is never easy. However, it is worth remembering that the rewards – particularly for those in the lead – are usually as rich as the journey is hard.

* * *

Turkeys Won't Vote for Christmas

Today, many IT departments do two things. Firstly they run a company's IT. And secondly, they try and tell everybody else what to do. The transition to cloud computing is therefore likely to have implications way beyond the IT department. Every computer user will be involved, and hence every business department. It is indeed for this reason that this chapter is called 'trouble in the boardroom'.

There is an old saying in computing that new developments are often held back by FUDGE. This stands for fear, uncertainty, doubt, greed and envy. Switching from in-house to cloud computing is likely to invoke all of these feelings in at least some staff. Indeed, over the next decade the cloud computing revolution is likely to prove quite an emotional rollercoaster. Many managers will be required to make leaps of faith, several traditional power bases and skills will be eroded, and lots of people will have to learn to work in new if more productive ways. Some people are likely to find the cloud computing revolution liberating and exciting, while for others there will be nothing but anguish and pain.

In the early days of the Internet revolution, a great many people used e-mail and the web at home before they did so at work. Today, Facebook, Twitter and other social networking sites have similarly introduced a large number of people to the power of collaborative cloud computing way ahead of its use in businesses. What this suggests is that companies need to quickly sit up and take notice. Online software and hardware can still go mainstream in business before the home if IT managers stop dragging their heels and adopt a more strategic perspective.

While many IT departments may prove somewhat resistant to cloud computing, I do not want to end this chapter being too negative about IT staff. Such individuals are, after all, expected to play out their working lives against a backdrop of constant revolution unknown in any other arena. No other professional needs to mentally and technically re-skill as often as those in the IT department. For a company's IT staff, embracing the cloud can therefore not be easy.

One of the reasons that IT professionals often fight the advancement of the cloud is explained by the inevitable divide between amateurs and professionals. Amateurs – such as home computing enthusiasts – tend to get excited by things that work. In contrast, professionals – such as those who run company IT systems – have to be more concerned with fixing things that do not. To take a broader example, an amateur photographer may take ten photos and be pleased with the single one that comes out well. In contrast, a professional photographer would soon be out of business if every one of her final client pictures was not of reasonable quality.

Professionals cannot ignore actual and possible problems the way that amateurs freely can. This means that it will often be amateurs who first experiment with new IT developments like cloud computing. What this also means is that anybody interested in cloud computing needs to pay at least some attention to what is happening in the consumer and amateur realm. In the next chapter we are therefore going to explore the personal cloud.

9

THE PERSONAL CLOUD

The final chapter of a book ought to wrap things up in a profound and heavyweight manner. Because of this, I have always considered it courteous for a book's penultimate chapter to offer a little light relief! This particular second-to-last chapter focuses on some of the more innovative and wacky ways in which cloud computing is starting to impact on our personal lives. So, you may ask, is this chapter a kind of dumping ground for fun material that did not slot in nicely anywhere else? Yes, absolutely it is! And I make no apology for that.

Digital sharing and communication have already become a mainstream human activity. In September 2009, Internet WorldStats.com estimated the global online population to be over 1.7 billion. Of these, about 400 million people were active users of Facebook, with about 200 million members checking the site every day. Every day YouTube plays out over one billion videos, while Twitter users post over fifty million tweets. In South Korea – the most wired nation on the planet – boot camps have even been established to cure children of Internet addiction. The cloud may be where businesses will soon run their applications and store their data. However, the online realm is without doubt already the most popular human playground and community space of all time.

Social networking sites including Facebook, MySpace and Twitter now provide the platforms on which many people run their social lives. The cloud can also provide individuals with all kinds of free software, as well as a secure place to store their digital stuff. In addition, the cloud is the frontier for next-generation computer games, as well as the stage for a new breed of online celebrity.

The personal cloud is already a very crowded and chaotic part of cyberspace. The extent to which some of us are populating it with all manner of personal data is also starting to raise significant privacy concerns. Many large and small companies now compete for our data and attention in the personal cloud. However, none of them is in control and probably none of them ever will be. The personal cloud is both amazing and anarchic, and at the same time worrying and wonderful. So let's jump right in and take a closer look.

The Rise and Rise of Online Social Networking

Social networking was the first truly mainstream cloud activity. In October 2009, market-research firm ComScore estimated that over 800 million people were regularly visiting a social networking site. As reported by researchers at Nielsen, since February 2009 people have begun to spend more time on social networking sites than using e-mail. How social networking will continue to evolve as the cloud matures is therefore a very common question. While nobody can provide a definitive answer, there are some trends and websites that perhaps provide a clue.

Today, a great many social networking site users have embraced multi-device access. In other words, people are accessing Bebo, Ning, Friendster, Twitter, LinkedIn,

Facebook and their ilk on mobile phones as well as desktop and laptop PCs. Whereas in business employees do not want to be separated from their e-mail, in our personal lives it is social networking site access that we cannot be without. We should therefore expect social networking users to take rapid advantage of developments in the device cloud as illustrated on page 132.

Already people are checking Facebook on tablets, nettop boxes and even surface computers. Accessing tweets on the cuffs of an online jacket or watching a YouTube video on the front of an Internet T-shirt is also quite likely late in this decade. Mashups of fashion and social networking may indeed one day be the Next Big Thing!

In addition to any time, any place and anywhere access, social networking content is increasingly being mashed and interlinked. Using real-time aggregator websites, people can now pull all of their social networking and social media content together in one place. For example, Friendfeed.com allows anybody to monitor real-time content from over fifty sites including Facebook, Twitter, Blogger, Flickr and Gmail. For those keen on presenting an up-to-date online profile, Naymz.com similarly allows the amalgamation of content from a number of other sites, including YouTube, LinkedIn and Twitter. It even gives each user a reputation score!

Video and social networking are also increasingly natural partners. YouTube already allows users to 'share their actions'. For example, when somebody rates or comments on a video this can be reflected on their channel homepage, as well as being automatically posted to Twitter or Facebook. The social networking site 12seconds.tv has also been designed exclusively to share 'video moments' of up to twelve seconds in duration. These tiny videos are recorded directly to the site from a webcam or mobile phone. They can then be shared as 'video status updates' on Twitter and Facebook.

Another trend is for social networking sites dedicated to particular activities. For example, Kaboodle.com describes itself as 'a social shopping community where people discover, recommend and share products'. Taking a different kind of approach, Squidoo.com allows users to create subject-specific overview pages or 'lenses' that others can then follow to keep up with a specialist topic.

Social networking sites are also increasingly likely to know where we are. This has already led to developments such as Foursquare, a location-based social networking and gaming site accessed from a mobile device. Users of Foursquare check in as they explore a city. They can also integrate their Twitter or Facebook accounts, and earn points when they discover new places.

By taking GPS readings, Foursquare and competitors including Gowalla and Brightkite allow people to know where their friends are and what they are doing. The Apple iPhone application Stalqer even tracks the location of somebody's friends via GPS in real-time. Not everybody may consider it 'awesome' for their friends and possibly others to be able to locate them on a map every minute of the day. However, both technically and in practice, such location-based social networking is already a reality.

Social networking and augmented reality are also beginning to merge. Already some smartphones running the Layar augmented reality browser can overlay social networking content on a handset's video feed. By just pointing such a smartphone at a building, a user can therefore see the tweets being written within. Even more amazingly, we will fairly soon be able to aim a mobile device at a room full of people and see social networking feeds overlaid. No really, we will!

The first augmented reality application that allows us to learn about a stranger simply by pointing a smartphone at them is called Recognizr. Developed by Swedish mobile phone company The Astonishing Tribe, the prototype software was premiered at the Mobile World Congress in Barcelona in February 2010. Recognizr uses a facial recognition application in a cloud data centre to identify people. It then aggregates social networking information that is overlaid in real-time on an augmented reality display. On screen, clickable data feeds from sites including Twitter, YouTube and Facebook literally hover above people's heads. This kind of development has now been labelled 'augmented identity'. If it ever takes hold, we may never have to talk to somebody we know nothing about ever again!

Personal Cloud Applications

Back in chapter three we looked at a range of online software applications including cloud word processors, spreadsheets, databases, photo and video editors, and website creators. Any individual with a computer and a web connection can now use a whole host of such cloud applications for free. It is therefore likely that within a few years most private individuals will never have to pay for software.

Free cloud software is already allowing individuals to use powerful applications at home that were once solely the preserve of big business. This means that clubs, charities and parent associations can now collaborate online and manage tasks that were previously beyond their scope and budget. For example, Google Sites now offers a fantastic tool for building a great free website with social tools, while Zoho Creator and Force.com offer anybody fantastic free online database functionality. Online scrapbooks, such as Zoho Notebook as illustrated on page 58, are also great free tools for aggregating all manner of text, images, audio and video content.

Private individuals can now also use free online software to do things that businesses would probably not be interested in. For example, one of the most fun new online applications of 2009 was Xtranormal.com. This allows anybody to create a 3D movie in real-time just by selecting characters and typing in what they want them to say.

Several free online tools have also been designed to help us run our lives more easily. For example, Zoho Planner can create cloud-based to-do lists, notes and reminders. Available from planner.zoho.com, it also allows friends to share photos. As an alternative, rememberthemilk.com is a simple online to-do list application. With a friendly cow logo, it can integrate with a range of other cloud services including Twitter and Google Calendar.

Lastly, a great many sites now allow us to do wacky things with digital media. For example, at liftmagic.com you can upload a photo and experiment with a wide range of cosmetic surgery treatments. Over at either writeonit.org or magmypic.com you can also place yourself on a magazine cover. While such effects are possible in a sophisticated online photo editor like Pixlr.com, dedicated websites make these kinds of media tricks very easy and addictive. Just don't try them when you are cooking dinner or things will end up getting burnt.

Fun and Games in the Cloud

As we all know, a great many non-business software applications are games. Indeed globally, more money is now spent on computer games than DVDs. As the cloud computing revolution unfolds, it is therefore inevitable that it will have a big impact on computer gaming.

Cloud computing will allow computer games to evolve in two ways. Firstly, developments in location-based tracking and augmented reality will allow computer games to be played out in the real world. Secondly, online hardware will also allow the 3D worlds in which many people roam, build and fight to be more sophisticated. We will also be able to play these more complex 3D games on lower-power computers.

Location-based computer games have already arrived. As mentioned a few pages back, in Foursquare, Gowalla and Brightkite players earn points by checking in when they visit real locations. Booyah's MyTown has even taken this concept a step further in a mashup of location-based gaming and Monopoly. When MyTown players arrive at a location they can not only check in, but also purchase it. This then allows them to earn virtual rent from other players.

Augmented reality developments are also starting to enable more sophisticated interactions with the real world. Using GPS and compass data from a mobile device, some augmented reality games already superimpose 2D or 3D graphics on real locations. This allows players to roam around a real city collecting virtual treasure or fighting virtual monsters. Virtual perils are also now being overlaid on real locations. For example, Firefighter 360 for the iPhone 3GS allows players to fight virtual fires in the real world. As well as augmented reality flames and water, the game even includes virtual screaming victims. It can be downloaded for $0.99.

For those who want to play computer games in the privacy of their own home, online processing power will enable new levels of realism. Today, some of the most highly specified home PCs are mainly used for playing games. This is because a great deal of processor power is needed to render the increasingly detailed 3D worlds that gamers demand. However, the use of online processing power will remove this processor overhead. Pretty soon we will therefore be playing games that look far better than those we have today, yet on lower-power computers and even mobile devices.

One of the first companies to capitalize on cloud-based gaming is a start-up called OnLive. OnLive runs high-performance games on its cloud servers. Its customers then access these games using an OnLive Microconsole connected to a television or on an entry-level desktop computer. The principle is exactly the same as running an online word processor on a Google or Zoho server. As OnLive's founder and CEO Steve Perlman explains:

> With OnLive we've cleared the last remaining hurdle for the video games industry: effective online distribution. By putting the value back into the games themselves and removing the reliance on expensive, short-lived hardware, we are dramatically shifting the economics of the industry.

OnLive has established partner agreements with Electronic Arts, Ubisoft, Warner Bros, Atari and other major games publishers to offer their existing high-performance titles from its website. You can find out more at onlive.com.

Nobody has yet announced a next-generation computer game that could never be installed on a stand-alone computer. However, for multi-player games in particular, the potential is highly significant. Current multi-player 3D games, such as EVE, require each user to run software on a PC that has to generate the games world locally. However, it will be far more efficient to generate awesome 3D worlds just once in a cloud data centre and then stream them out over the Internet to thousands of players.

Storing Our Digital Stuff

For individuals, one of the greatest benefits of cloud computing is that it can provide somewhere safe to store valued digital content. Almost all online applications keep a user's data safe in the cloud. However, there are also a wide range of cloud services for storing and sharing documents, photos, music, videos and all manner of digital files. As a very popular example, many people now keep and share their photos on Flickr.com.

While businesses may harbour concerns about the security of files uploaded online, private individuals ought to realize that data held in the cloud is likely to be far safer than any file kept on a local PC, laptop or hard disk. At home, a fire, burglary or hardware failure can permanently prevent access to an individual's documents or photo album with a great deal of irreplaceable material and sentimental value being lost. Granted, care needs to be taken when uploading financial, legal or other sensitive documents to the cloud. However, for most people most of the time, the crucial point about our digital filestore is that it remains available for the rest of our lives.

Cloud storage services come in two flavours. Some simply provide online filespace, while others also include a back-up synchronization service. An online filespace can be thought of as a hard disk in the cloud that can be accessed with a web browser to upload or download files. One example of such a service is Microsoft's Windows Live Skydrive, available from skydrive.live.com. This provides 25Gb of personal storage absolutely free, if with an individual file size limit of 50Mb. As an alternative, Google Docs offers 1Gb of free online storage to which any kind of file can be uploaded up to a maximum size also of 1Gb. Google then charge $5 a year for each additional 20Gb. Files stored on either Skydrive or Google Docs can remain private or may be publicly or privately shared.

Another popular online filespace provider is box.net. Again 1Gb of storage is provided for free. However, individuals then have to pay $9.95 a month for 10Gb. Microsoft's free 25Gb on Skydrive or Google's offer of $5 per 20Gb a year to keep digital content on its servers therefore remain difficult to ignore.

For those people who may forget to regularly back up their data to Skydrive or Google Docs, there are cloud storage services that automate the process. These require the installation of a piece of software on each computer that uses them. This local application then automatically backs up data to the cloud, and may also synchronize it across PCs. Such a service is offered by dropbox.com, which describes itself as a kind of 'magic pocket' that becomes available on all of your devices and online. Many other companies offer a similar service. These include livedrive.com, who even claim to provide 'absolutely unlimited' online back-up for $3.95 a month. As a third alternative, CloudBerryLab.com provide a range of easy-to-use consumer web interfaces for Amazon's mighty Simple Storage Service (S3) as detailed back in chapter four.

The Rise of the Cloud Celebrity

With more and more people now consuming online media, opportunities are starting to arise for a whole new species of cloud celebrity. In the noughties, some members of the public achieved a little fame and fortune by taking part in a reality TV show. However today, global stardom and payouts from online advertising are within the potential reach of anybody with an Internet connection.

One of the first cloud celebrities is Justine Ezarik, otherwise known online as iJustine. On her website at ijustine.com, the attractive, twenty-something blonde describes herself as a 'video blogger, Internet personality, Apple geek, YouTuber, designer and a tech addict!' These are also all the things at which she has become remarkably proficient.

iJustine is highly active on Twitter and Facebook, regularly posts pictures on DailyBooth and Flickr, and runs three closely interlinked YouTube channels. These contain her own music and satirical videos, plus technology reviews and a 'You Can Ask iJ' series in which she answers questions posted by fans. In total the 550+ videos iJustine has uploaded to YouTube have obtained over 85 million views. iJustine also has nearly 500,000 subscribers to her YouTube channels and over 1.1 million followers on Twitter.

Anybody trying to work out how to use the cloud to obtain fame or fortune ought to study iJustine. At first glance, the majority of her videos and other content appear simple, off-the-cuff and run-of-the-mill. But they are not. For a start, everything iJustine uploads always contains at least one explicit question. These encourage fans to leave comments, hence pushing her videos up YouTube's rating system and increasing her video hits and advertising revenue. iJustine's use of annotated overlays to link videos together is also very effective. On top of all this, she has launched a merchandising website to sell user-customizable iJustine 'T-shirts, goodies and stuff'.

Described by Wikipedia as a 'viral videocomedienne' and 'lifecasting star', iJustine is a great example of a cloud celebrity and self-made online brand. Everything she does in the cloud is fun but also clearly calculated to maximize views and subscriptions. As she writes on one of her channels, 'I make videos here on YouTube and I hope you like them. If you don't, maybe you should watch a few more?' In one of her tweets she once typed that she 'loves Twitter more than probably my own child if I had one'. And maybe this says it all.

It is also not only hot blondes with decent video editing

skills who are achieving celebrity status in the cloud. Perhaps surprisingly, academics are also playing the game. For example, Michael Wesch, as Assistant Professor of Cultural Anthropology in Kansas State University, has become famous for producing YouTube videos about the impact of new media. The first of these, called 'Web 2.0 ... The Machine is Us/ing Us', has now been viewed over eleven million times and has earned Professor Wesch a Rave Award from *Wired* magazine.

Another academic who has achieved a significant level of cloud celebrity is Professor Martyn Poliakoff from the University of Nottingham. Professor Poliakoff is the presenter of the 'Periodic Table of Videos'. With over seven million views, this online series features a YouTube movie about each of the 118 chemical elements. As a result of his online fame, Professor Poliakoff has held video tutorials with school children and other online chemistry fans from around the world. You can watch him demonstrating chemistry online at periodicvideos.com.

Privacy and the Personal Cloud

In February 2010, a website called PleaseRobMe.com highlighted the potential dangers of sharing too much personal information online. Created in just a few hours by three Dutch web developers, the site extracts information from Foursquare players who have chosen to share their real-world location publicly via Twitter. It then indicates when their homes are empty.

Despite the name, PleaseRobMe.com is not intended as a burglary tool. Rather, as one of its creators explained to the BBC, the point is to get across that 'not long ago it was questionable to share your full name on the Internet. [And now] we've gone past that point by 1,000 miles.' Nobody would sensibly put a sign on their door saying 'I am out' when they leave their house. However, many people now broadcast such information far more publicly on Twitter and related websites.

Other valuable personal information is also commonly left lying around online. For example, as mentioned in chapter five, many Facebook users list their favourite places, colours and films on the site. While this may not sound like a security risk, if such information is also used in passwords or as website account 'memorable information' then it is very foolish indeed. Today most people really do need to start taking far more care of their identity and personal information when they venture online.

Unfortunately, even when individuals are careful, online privacy can be breached by the careless or even intentional exploits of cloud service providers. Most alarmingly in recent times, there were massive personal privacy breaches when Google added the 'Buzz' social networking functionality to its Gmail cloud e-mail service in February 2010. What Google did was to configure Buzz to automatically generate a group of friends to follow. This follower list was based on each user's most frequent e-mail contacts. By default it was also shared with all of a user's automatically generated friends. As a result, some journalists ended up sharing their exceedingly private, off-the-record contacts with one another. Some people having affairs also found that each partner suddenly knew the identity of their other lovers! While Google acted rapidly to sort this problem out, it could inevitably not undo some of the damage.

Mistakes aside, some big-name cloud service providers actively seek to obtain the rights to our personal information. Perhaps most alarmingly, Facebook claims a 'transferable, sub-licensable, royalty-free, world-wide license' to use any photographic or video content uploaded to the site. Most users may be utterly unaware of this.

However, the statement online at facebook.com/terms.php is quite clear.

While the value of most people's photos and videos may appear minimal, due to cloud computing developments this will not necessarily remain the case. For example, good vision recognition systems – such as those necessary to enable the augmented identity systems discussed earlier in this chapter – will require access to vast image databases that contain as many pictures as possible of a great many individuals. The more images that are in these databases, the more likely it is that vision recognition systems will be able to identify people. The fact that Facebook already has the right to license the use of over ten billion photos uploaded to its site may therefore be highly significant.

*   *   *

The Cyborg Emerges?
Back in 2003, Sherry Turkle – a professor at the world-famous Massachusetts Institute of Technology (MIT) – wrote that 'in our culture, technology has moved from being a tool to a prosthetic to become part of our cyborg selves'. What she was implying was that technological devices are no longer something we just pick up to help us achieve one task. Nor are our technologies still distinctly separable from our 'natural' selves. Rather, many of us have already 'fused' with smartphones and other cloud access devices to such an extent that they have well and truly become part of our being. Some people now panic when they cannot find their mobile phone. A few individuals even exhibit severe emotional distress if their phone is broken or when they do not have access to the Internet.

In the second decade of the twenty-first century many people already live part of their lives online. The digital footprints that most of us cast in the personal cloud are also becoming a valuable source of information. Every time we go online we surrender a little piece of ourselves. It is indeed already impossible to conduct a web search, visit a social networking site, watch an online video, use an online application, or make an online purchase, without leaving a digital trail. Our cloud activities already allow online systems to learn about us and to predict our desires in a manner that may save us frustration, money and time. However, a surveillance-heavy society is also emerging in which our activities, thoughts and locations are a little less private than they were even a decade ago.

Many of those who study the application and development of the Internet tend to focus on privacy loss and the negative implications of the personal cloud. This is also rather sad. Undoubtedly the Internet has become 'contaminated' with Big Business since the commercial use of the web was first permitted back in the early 1990s. However, there are also many benefits that continue to arise from our mass digital interconnection and online knowledge sharing.

Cloud computing is the latest phase of an online revolution that is continuing to permit private individuals to learn, communicate, collaborate and establish business ventures in new ways. As a consequence, cloud computing is already allowing ordinary citizens to achieve things that they could not accomplish before. Over the next decade cloud computing may prove painful for the traditional computing industry and many internal IT departments. However, as we shall see in the next and final chapter, the future of the cloud is likely to be far more positive than negative for private individuals and humanity as a whole.

10

CLOUD COMPUTING IN THE FUTURE

Sixteen years ago I started writing a book called *Cyber Business* that predicted the rise of the Internet as a mainstream business and social tool. Today, I am finishing writing a book about cyber business in practice. We may now call it cloud computing. However, the idea has not changed one bit.

Since I started writing this book the US Airforce has signed a cloud computing deal with IBM. Layar have also announced the first commercial augmented reality app store, while Google has released Google Googles, the first visual search application. Not to be outdone, Apple has launched its highly anticipated iPad tablet to provide a new means of accessing the cloud. Microsoft has even 'gone cloud' with a new cloud services website, the launch of its Azure platform, and the announcement of Microsoft Office Web Apps.

The above and the many other cloud-related launches and announcements of late 2009 and early 2010 signal how cloud computing has come of age. With even Microsoft now on-side, the scepticism towards cloud computing exhibited by many in 2008 and 2009 has given way to an admittedly sometimes mournful realism. Like it or not, we are all now part of the cloud computing steamroller or the traditional computing road.

As discussed throughout this book, cloud computing is where software, hardware, data and artificial intelligence are accessed from the Internet using any kind of computing device. Cloud computing is also very much the future. This said, by the end of the decade the label 'cloud computing' will probably have disappeared. In the same way that 'business' and 'e-business' are now accepted as the same thing, so fairly soon 'computing' and 'cloud computing' will simply be synonymous.

In what is sadly the last chapter of this book, I am going to consider where cloud computing is headed in the future. OK, so I do not have a crystal ball. However, as a professional futurist I have grown used to the criticisms often levelled at those of us who attempt to future gaze. There are after all only two certainties in life. The first is death. The second is that until we die we will spend the rest of our days living in the future. The extrapolation of probable tomorrows based on a knowledge of the cutting-edge of today ought therefore to be of some interest to us all.

Unlimited Power on Tap

For the best part of three decades the majority of computer users have demanded and obtained increasingly powerful PCs and laptops. However, once cloud computing goes mainstream, the pursuit of end-user computing power will well and truly come to an end. From a user perspective, one of the really great things about cloud computing is that it will soon enable any kind of computing device to access as much processing power and storage capacity as it requires. The practically unlimited computing power soon to be available from the cloud will also allow us to achieve many currently impossible things.

Within five years we will be able to use PCs, laptops, netbooks, TVs, tablets and even smartphones to run photorealistic computer games and visit virtual reality worlds. We will also be able to edit video and show the final product in real-time on any kind of cloud access device. Waiting an hour or two for a PC to create a DVD or Blu-Ray disk of a home movie will be a thing of the past. Not, of course, that we will be watching DVDs or Blu-Ray disks! Rather, most videos – be they personal or commercial – will soon be out in the cloud. YouTube already handles high-definition video and hosts an increasing variety of full-length TV shows. Most major broadcasters now also provide access to current and archive programmes via their websites. Cloud computing will therefore soon allow us to watch any film or TV show we want on any cloud access device we carry or visit.

Constant access to the power of a cloud data centre will also allow any computer to be equipped with sophisticated voice and vision recognition. This will permit the real-time translation of human speech into any language. Indeed, Google have already indicated that a cloud-based spoken language translation service will be available on its smartphones within a few years. This literally means that we will be able to speak English into a smartphone and have Mandarin, German, Russian or whatever language we choose come out at the other end.

Cloud-based vision recognition also means that we will be able to hold up any computing device and have it instantly recognize whatever we are looking at and provide more information. Augmented reality is already the poster-child of new cloud computing applications. It is also likely to remain so for a few years to come. However, in the future augmented reality displays will not only be featured on smartphones, tablets and similar mobile devices.

Already there are prototypes of vehicle-based augmented reality systems. These project data and graphics on to the windscreen, hence allowing direction arrows and other information to appear overlaid on the road. General Motors is already working with several universities to develop this technology.

By the end of the decade we may also be able to view augmented reality through contact lenses linked to the cloud. As reported by bionanotechnology expert Babak A. Parviz, contact lenses with simple built-in electronics are already being produced in small numbers in his laboratory at the University of Washington. These prototypes feature a very simple LED display matrix capable of superimposing a single letter on the real world. While the resolution is currently crude, the prototype lenses already feature wireless power and wireless networking. They could also be developed to allow a high-quality video image to be superimposed on top of our natural vision.

It is now reasonable to suggest that contact lenses with an integrated computer display will be able to be wirelessly linked to a camera, compass and GPS locator worn elsewhere on the body. Future contact lenses could therefore become fully functional augmented reality cloud access devices. The implications of this are also profound. For example, in future surgeons may be able to see augmented reality MRI scan and other real-time medical data overlaid on a patient while they are operating on them. The deaf may also be able to see the speech of anybody they are looking at overlaid as subtitles. Everybody walking down a street could also wear a virtual Twitter or Facebook icon. These could then be expanded by a hard stare followed by a rapid double-blink of the eyelids! More mundanely, we could watch television or view documents with our eyes closed.

While next decade the above may well be possible, many people are likely to get fed up with augmented reality at least some of the time. After all, coping with reality itself can be bad enough without having an extra one or several superimposed! However, cloud contact lens technology may even help us deal with visual overload by permitting the development of diminished reality (DR).

Suppose, for example, that there are things around us that we really do not want to see. These could include advertisements, graffiti, rubbish or even screaming children in the park. No problem. Future diminished reality systems could use cloud processing power to recognize the things that we do not want to view. Vision processing web services would then be applied to retouch the view from our eyes in real-time, so removing all unwanted elements from our vision. We would, of course, have to be careful about what we chose to have erased. For example, making traffic on the road invisible would almost certainly not be very smart! However, thanks in part to the virtually unlimited cloud processing power that will in future be available to us, rose-tinted diminished reality contact lenses do remain a theoretical possibility.

Very-Many-Core Cloud Processors

While the above scenarios may be many years away, the advancements in data centre technology that may permit them are starting to arrive today. In December 2009 Intel unveiled a prototype 'cloud processor' that could power the next generation of cloud data centre servers. Known as the single-chip cloud computer – or SCC – this contains forty-eight processing cores on a square of silicon about the size of a postage stamp. This is like having forty-eight server computers on a single chip. Another manufacturer called Tilera has already announced a 100-core processor. Within five years we may therefore see cloud server processors with many hundreds of cores.

Very-many-core processors will permit incredibly high densities of computing power to be concentrated into very small spaces. Indeed, by the end of the decade it is reasonable to suggest that a data centre with several million processor cores will be able to be housed in a space no bigger than an average house. While this may lead some to conclude that computing power will remain local, this is not likely to be the case. Rather, very-many-core processors will make it obvious that only large cloud vendors will be able to manage computer power in an economic and environmentally friendly manner.

An individual computer with a very-many-core processor could perform almost any computing task that a user could throw at it in real-time. However, a very-many-core core processor running in an end-user computing device or even in most company data centres would almost always be powered but idle as it waited for something to process. In the near future, the carbon footprint of wasted computer power is also likely to become environmentally unacceptable.

Only in cloud data centres will very-many-core processors be able to be efficiently utilized. This is because they will always be able to be run at full capacity by sharing their considerable power among a great many users. Already, cloud computing data centres are becoming the power plants of the information age. Fairly soon, very-many-core processors will allow them to become our information age nuclear reactors. While few people will ever go near a very-many-core cloud processor, most of us will nevertheless access one a great many times each day.

The Cloud at Sea?

Even with these amazing processors at the heart of their servers, cloud data centres will consume very large amounts of electrical energy. As a result, cloud data centre carbon footprints are likely to be closely scrutinized. In anticipation of this, big cloud computing vendors are already seeking cheaper and cleaner forms of electricity. As noted in chapter one, Iceland is hoping that cloud vendors will relocate to its shores to power and cool their servers from its geothermal energy and natural abundance of cold. However, another green option may be the development of off shore, wave-powered data centres.

Google has already filed a patent for a 'floating platform-mounted computer data centre comprising a plurality of computing units, a sea-based electrical generator . . . [and] . . . one or more sea-water cooling units'. This patent was awarded in April 2009 and incorporates so-called 'Pelamis machine' pontoons that use wave motion to generate electrical power. Google has calculated that an array of pontoons spread over one square kilometre would produce the thirty megawatts of electricity necessary to run a floating data centre's servers. These would then be naturally cooled using seawater–freshwater heat exchangers, which would effectively turn the ocean into a giant heatsink.

The server computers in a floating data centre would be sealed in standard shipping containers. These would then be transported by truck and placed on the boat by crane. The plans in Google's patent envisage floating data centres moored three to seven miles out at sea. In theory this could mean that they would not incur any property taxes.

Offshore floating data centres could also raise interesting questions of legal jurisdiction. For example, which laws – if any – would govern the handling of cloud data managed from ships out at sea? In future, it may not just be oil tankers and ocean liners that exploit the option of sailing under a flag of convenience.

Crowdsourcing and Open Source Solutions

A floating data centre is an innovative idea that could help to significantly reduce computing's carbon footprint. It is also the kind of innovative thinking that the human race will need far more of in the face of global challenges that include dwindling natural resources, rising industrialization and over-population.

Because it enables computer power to be efficiently centralized, cloud computing is already being heralded as a future solution rather than a future problem. However, by facilitating new forms of collaboration and data sharing, cloud computing may also play a far broader role in helping to shape a more positive tomorrow.

Already cloud computing is providing the backbone for a new, collective human activity known as 'crowdsourcing'. This is where value is created by using the Internet to obtain and share inputs from a great many people. As discussed in chapter two, individuals can now pool their collective intelligence by using online tools to very rapidly and effectively collaborate. Already the blogs, videos and tweets of citizen journalists help the news to go global in real-time and prevent most governments from hiding the truth. As collaborative cloud computing tools go mainstream, we should similarly anticipate the rising influence of global citizen thinkers who use the Internet to collectively brainstorm fresh ideas.

It is becoming increasingly common for intellectual property to be developed and hosted online in the public domain. This trend started with the development of 'open source' software by groups of programmers who freely share all aspects of their work. Open source allows for the public creation of programs far too complex for any one individual to code, as well as for their testing and constant improvement. One major example of open source software is the Linux operating system that now forms the basis of Google Chrome OS. Other examples include the Firefox web browser and the popular free word processing, spreadsheet and presentations application OpenOffice.

It is, however, not just software that is already being created by individuals who adhere to the open source philosophy and freely share their intellectual property online. Some physical products are now also being developed in this fashion. One example is the RepRap – or Replicating Rapid-prototyper – a 3D printer capable of copying itself by printing out its own components. This is being developed by a community over at reprap.org, and where all designs and instructions for building a RepRap are available for free. There is also a similar project called Fab@Home. This can be found at fabathome.org.

Even more ambitiously, there are now several projects leveraging the collaborative power of the cloud to design and build open source vehicles. These include OScar (www.theoscarproject.org), which is part of the Open Source Green Vehicle project (OSGV). While OScar is in its early stages, another initiative called the Riversimple Open Source Hydrogen Car Project has already produced a prototype vehicle that has been driven (see riversimple.com). There are currently also several open source initiatives intent on producing better prosthetic limbs (such as that at openprosthetics.org), as well as many focused on the development of open source robots.

The Rise of Open Data
The open source philosophy of developing and publishing valuable information online may become one of the greatest

benefits of the cloud. Projects to share so-termed 'open data' are also already springing up around the world. For example, in early 2010 the UK government launched a website called data.gov.uk to open up a wealth of its data for reuse.

One of those working on the data.gov.uk project is Tim Berners-Lee, the guy who invented the world wide web in the first place. His intention is to allow the more effective interlinking of data across different boundaries, hence enabling the development of new knowledge and innovative cloud applications. In this context, data.gov.uk is indeed a new kind of crowdsourcing forum for generating ideas and mashing new applications from a mass of free public data. As an aside, it also happens to be hosted on Amazon Web Services.

Anybody can use the data available at data.gov.uk for any private or commercial purpose. Scores of new applications have already been created. These include Find GPs (which enables people to locate a doctor on their iPhone), Parkopedia (which assists in finding somewhere to park), Where Can I Live? (which tells people where they can afford to buy a property), the Renewable Energy Map, and the vast Gazetteer for Scotland encyclopaedia.

The Monitoring of People and Things
Crowdsourcing has typically involved people consciously collaborating in open source initiatives or mashing open data. However, this does not have to be the case. Increasingly, crowdsourcing is also starting to allow value to be generated from the unconscious contributions we all make to the cloud.

Today most people cast an online data shadow. This digital footprint of our lives grows every time we use a search engine, visit Facebook, send an e-mail or a tweet, use a SaaS application, make an online purchase, watch a

YouTube video, or in fact do anything else on the Internet. Once online face recognition takes hold – and it will be with us sooner than you think – every time we walk down the street or are snapped on a smartphone we will also be logged in one cloud data centre or another.

The above is the current reality. However, in the future our data shadows may rapidly extend as cloud technology permits the automatic monitoring of practically every object we purchase, manipulate or discard. This means that even when we are not using a cloud access device we may still be extending our digital footprint and allowing others to crowdsource value from our activity.

Until recently the only way to put an object online was to provide it with its own Internet connection, or at the very least a bar code or radio frequency identification (RFID) tag that would allow it to be monitored. However, cloud-based vision recognition will soon change all this by turning almost every camera into a cloud computing data capture device.

As the Google Goggles visual search application already highlights, all that is really needed to put an object online is for a cloud data centre to know what it looks like. Indeed, as soon as an object can be recognized by an online camera it starts to cast its own data shadow each and every time it is viewed. In turn this information may be linked to the activity of a human being. Already the progress of vehicles on some major roads is monitored by cameras that read their number plates and record a data shadow of their journey. Drivers of any vehicles that speed may then automatically be sent tickets.

In addition to cameras, an increasing number of devices will fairly soon be able to directly or indirectly track human activity and relay it to the cloud. For example, smart electricity meters will have an Internet connection. Some of these can already identify when specific electrical items are turned on or off by recognizing their power signature. Many people and objects may also start to share GPS data on their location. Indeed it is likely that in five years' time every mobile computing device will know where it is and will be capable of relaying that information.

Due to the above developments, many of the items we buy are in the future likely to cast a trackable data shadow. The cradle-to-grave monitoring of the things we consume may even become an environmental necessity that allows for the levy of individual carbon taxes. In the future, cameras in supermarkets may monitor what items are taken off the shelf and by whom. Public CCTV cameras could then monitor us back home where our fridges and bins would log our purchases in and out. The potential is therefore emerging for a data shadow to be cast by pretty much every one of our daily activities.

The real-time monitoring of the data shadows of both ourselves and the things we consume and otherwise manipulate may prove highly beneficial. For example, it could eliminate waste by allowing manufacturers and supermarkets to very accurately predict what food they need to produce, transport and stock. It could also save energy by allowing the augmented reality windscreens in our cars to take account of all other traffic and direct us the most efficient way home. However, we also need to recognize the potentially negative consequences that may arise as cloud data centres become part of an all-seeing surveillance apparatus or 'panopticon'.

The Emerging Cloud Panopticon

The idea of a panoptic structure was first conceived in the eighteenth century by the moral philosopher Jeremy Bentham. He envisaged panopticons as prisons or other institutions within which every inmate could be subject to constant observation. Bentham's plans were put into effect in Russia in 1787 when a polygon-shaped factory was built around a central watchtower. Mirrors were also positioned to provide additional lines of sight. Those in control at the top of the watchtower therefore had every opportunity to continually observe workers.

Within Jeremy Bentham's panoptic factory a state of 'universal transparency' was achieved. This means that the workers in the factory knew that they laboured within an environment where permanent surveillance was possible. As a result the workers became more placid. The power of a panoptic structure to change human behaviour was thereby demonstrated. What we need to appreciate today is that by embracing the cloud we are almost certainly crafting a new global panopticon that is similarly likely to change human behaviour.

Anybody who writes an e-mail in Gmail or Hotmail ought to be aware that their message will be scanned. This occurs to allow Google or Microsoft to provide the sender with individually targeted advertising. Information on our web searches is also stored by Google for a short period of time. As discussed in chapter two, whenever we visit a Web 2.0 site like YouTube or Facebook our individual actions also lead to associations that help tailor future content for both ourselves and other users. Whether we think about it or not, we are already monitored every time we touch an online keyboard or mouse. In this sense a cloud-based panopticon has already arrived. All that the developments covered in this chapter will therefore do is to widen the cloud panopticon's scope and scale.

Today most of us still have the choice of whether or not we want to cloud compute. However, once cameras and other sensors become cloud input devices this will no longer be the case. This said, constant monitoring within the cloud panopticon is not necessarily something we should fear. After all, in many public spaces cameras are welcomed and make people feel more safe. Quite possibly, our fear of crime and crime itself will in future fall quite sharply once public CCTV cameras are monitored by vision recognition systems in cloud data centres. Today a criminal caught on camera still has a significant chance of evading the law. However, while human operators cannot keep an eye on everything and everybody, a cloud data centre will be able to keep track of every one of us whenever we venture into a public space. This means that future criminals caught on camera will be very likely to be apprehended. In turn this may cause them to think twice before offending in the first place.

Being monitored by the cloud will almost inevitably change most people's behaviour a little. However, if it alters our patterns of consumption this may be no bad thing. Cloud computing will not only help us save energy, but will also monitor our waste and inform others of our actions. If this means that individuals and businesses start to waste less, then future generations at least may give the cloud panopticon a cheer.

Web Squared and Thinking in the Cloud

In October 2009, the sixth Web 2.0 Summit was held in San Francisco. At this event Web 2.0 pioneers Tim O'Reilly and John Battelle noted how innovations like vision recognition will soon lead to an exponential growth in the volume of data processed and stored in the cloud. As a consequence, they suggested that we now ought to talk not of 'Web 2.0' but of 'Web-to-the-power-two', or 'Web Squared'.

Given that O'Reilly came up with the term 'Web 2.0' in the first place, he has some significant personal incentive in trying to label the Next Big Thing. However, in their powerful white paper *Web Squared: Web 2.0 Five Years On*, O'Reilly and Battelle do make some interesting arguments. In particular, they suggest that we ought to think of the Internet as a newborn baby that can see but has yet to develop the ability to focus. They go on to describe how today the Internet is awash with sensations, few of which it currently understands. However, they predict that like a growing child, the Internet is starting to filter signal from the mass of noisy data to which it is daily subjected. They also suggest that the web is destined to get smarter and smarter as it matures.

The picture on the front of this book suggests a computer thinking in the cloud. This image quite accurately reflects how computer applications, data and processing power are moving online. However, it also signals how local computers will soon start to tap into sophisticated pools of online artificial intelligence that will enable them to perform tasks such as vision and voice recognition. This means that quite literally our cloud access devices will start to think in the cloud. More than this, as online data shadows intermingle in crowdsourcing mashups – and as people increasingly collaborate and interlink online – so a single, planetary intelligence may be starting to emerge.

Intelligence may be defined as the ability to make sense of and respond to a mass of information. Clearly therefore, the more information an entity can store and process, the more likely it is to be able to develop intelligence. For years most work in the field of artificial intelligence has focused on making individual computing devices smart. However, given how little information about the world any single computing device is likely to be able to store and process, such an approach has to be somewhat flawed. The individual device approach is also unnecessary now that cloud computing has arrived. If sentient artificial intelligence ever does emerge it will be born not on one device, but in a cloud data centre nourished by crowdsourced information supplied by us all.

The idea that the world wide web will become the world's first sentient artificial intelligence is already a cliché. It is also an idea that misses the point. With their Web Squared concept, O'Reilly and Battelle are proposing that a planetary-scale 'collective mind' is starting to emerge. However, they are not suggesting that this new being is entirely artificial. Rather, they are saying that people are beginning to interconnect online to such an extent that humanity itself is now starting to think collectively in the cloud. The Internet may be evolving into a planetary intelligence. However, as should be obvious every time we visit Facebook, YouTube or Twitter, we need to remember that the Internet is built not just from computer technology but from the contributions of us all.

In the post-credit-crunch, pre-oil-crash and pre-mass-scarcity world of the early twenty-first century, humanity faces a great many challenges. These challenges are also global and have to addressed on a global scale. No nation can tackle climate change, pending fresh water shortages or the development of the greener energy and transportation technologies that we so desperately require. However, open source developments like those mentioned earlier in this chapter do already suggest the green shoots of possible solutions. The negative side of cloud computing is that we all end up surrendering and investing some of our very selves into the cloud. However, the very positive side of cloud computing is exactly the same. The rise of a crowdsourced collective mind interlinking the majority of human beings has to offer the hope for a brighter and more sustainable tomorrow. Those who have so quickly built the web have almost certainly shown us the way. The tools of cloud computing are increasingly in our hands. All we have to do is to use them.

The End of Individual Property?
The Web Squared white paper by Tim O'Reilly and John Battelle is well worth a read. You can download it for free from web2summit.com. As it argues, the world wide web is now on a 'collision course with the physical world'. In turn, this 'opens enormous new possibilities for business, and enormous new possibilities to make a difference on the world's most pressing problems'.

In a sense the world and the world wide web or 'the cloud' are becoming one and the same thing. This also has to occur. Or as the Web Squared white paper concludes:

> If we are going to solve the world's most pressing problems, we must put the power of the Web to work – its tech-nologies, its business models, and perhaps most importantly, its philosophies of openness, collective intelligence, and transparency . . . . Web meets World – that's Web Squared.

The developments in cloud computing explored throughout this book are fundamental to the broad concept of Web Squared and perhaps even to the evolution and survival of humanity. What this means is that the develop-ment of cloud computing cannot be seen or judged in isolation from far wider issues. Most significantly, embracing cloud computing is about letting go. In particular, it is about ceasing to build walls around our own things and casting aside many aspects of entirely individual physical possession.

We may like to have company data centres full of our own servers, as well as homes piled with CDs, DVDs and sheets of dead tree smeared with information. However, such a state of affairs is simply not sustainable. Fairly soon both local servers and multiple copies of media will have to disappear. The cloud will also allow this to happen. When a new movie comes out for home purchase, why do literally millions of plastic boxes need to be sold containing a disk also made from oil? Surely charging customers for the right to access a single, shared copy of the film uploaded to a cloud computing server is a far more environmentally friendly and sensible solution? Deep down we all know that it is. However, like using software and hardware in the cloud, it will take a bit of getting used to.

To be truly comfortable with cloud computing requires at least some acceptance of the folly of private property. We may be descended from hunter gatherers with the 'gatherer' part in us all still pretty strong. However, as we become more environmentally aware – and as we accept how wrong the bankers and the economists have got it for so long – so we will learn that all forms of property have to remain at least partly shared. The cloud is also the best development ever for allowing us to share things that can still in some respects remain our own.

Cloud computing is computing for a more joined-up, less defensive and less me-first world that has a chance of longer-term survival. Just as the PC revolution gave many individuals the freedom to create and communicate, so the cloud computing revolution will enable us all to engage in some new and very positive forms of collective thinking and accomplishment.

* * *

The Revolution Continues
This book has been written in the cloud. Across many months and hundreds of writing sessions I have also never

experienced a single problem. On no occasion has Google Docs ever crashed or been unavailable. I have also never needed to resort to a local back-up file. Indeed, once I learnt to press F11 and then <Ctrl><Shift><F> to hide every single menu and clear the entire screen for writing I was really cooking with gas!

My experience writing this book in Google Docs serves as a testament to the arrival of mainstream cloud computing. Few people really believed me when I told them I was going to write this book online. Yet that is exactly what I have done. My only regret is that I could not find an online equivalent of Adobe Illustrator in which to draw the figures, and that my chapters are now having to be downloaded to local software for typesetting.

Revolutions are a team sport. They therefore cannot gather their necessary momentum in a technologist's lab. In fact, by definition, revolutions require lots and lots of people to get involved. You. Me. The brunette down the street who wears a pink anorak. The quiet guy who walks his dog on a Sunday morning. The kids who play their computer games too loudly. And even the IT manager who does not want to say goodbye to his local servers. Like it or loathe it, a real revolution has to involve the majority.

The cloud computing revolution is just starting to take place right now. By reading this book you have, I hope, decided to become part of it. However, as you are well aware, participation requires more than exercising your grey matter to process some text. Exactly what your next steps ought to be also has to depend on who you are.

If you have management responsibility, then you need to help ensure that your organization has a cloud computing action plan like that featured in chapter seven. Alternatively, if you are an IT professional, then you need to rapidly learn far more about the technologies behind platform and infrastructure as a service. In part this is so you can help your current organization. However, just as importantly, such knowledge will prove critical in protecting and developing your own career.

If you are a student or somebody wishing to change their job, then you need to experiment with as many online software applications as possible. This can be done for nothing save the cost of your time and powering up a computer with an Internet connection. However, it will quickly allow you to present a CV or résumé that includes new skills to interest potential employers. Pretty much everybody these days advertises themselves with 'good IT skills in Microsoft Office'. However, to be a stand-out candidate over the next few years you ideally also need to be listing your ability to work with Google Docs, Zoho, Microsoft Web Apps, Acrobat.com and more.

Finally, if you are none of the above, you just need to get online and experiment – or as we used to say 'play' – with all of the great, free stuff that is out there in the cloud!

So here we are, at the end of *A Brief Guide to Cloud Computing*. Well OK, if you are really keen on a cover-to-cover experience you can now read the cloud computing directory, glossary and index. However, these are really only intended to be dipped into as required! If you want even more you can visit explainingcomputers.com/cloud where you will find videos and other online resources that highlight the key messages in this book. But this all said, this book really is now coming to an end.

I hope these pages have taught you a little about cloud computing. In fact, I hope they have taught you a lot! However, to really learn about cloud computing requires end-user experience. Telling somebody that they can word process, do their accounts or edit a movie online is one thing. Yet actually doing this is what creates cloud computing evangelists. So go on: if you have not done so already, dive in and join the religion. Visit a cloud computing website. And once there, dare to click.

CLOUD COMPUTING DIRECTORY

Listed below are all of the cloud applications and services covered in this book, with a few others thrown in for good measure. You can access an online and continually updated version of this directory from **explainingcomputers.com/ cloud**

Office Applications

Acrobat.com – acrobat.com
Acrobat.com is a suite of cloud services and applications from Adobe. These include a word processor named Buzzword, a spreadsheet called Tables, and a presentation package called Presentations. See page 57.

Google Apps – apps.google.com
Google Apps is a paid online office suite that includes Google Docs, Gmail, Google Calendar, Google Video private video hosting and the Google Sites website creation tool. By using the Google Apps Marketplace (see below), many other business software applications can also be integrated. See page 52.

Google Docs – docs.google.com

Google Docs is the free online word processor, spreadsheet, drawing and presentations package that was used to write this book. It has excellent collaborative tools, and includes a form generator for creating online surveys. See page 48.

Microsoft Office Web Apps – microsoft.com/office

Microsoft Office Web Apps are online versions of Microsoft Word, Excel, PowerPoint and OneNote. At the time of writing these applications were just about to be launched as one element of Office 2010. See page 59.

SlideRocket – sliderocket.com

SlideRocket is a very sophisticated online presentation package available in both free and subscription formats. SlideRocket presentations can include video and live data from other packages, including Google Docs. There is also an integrated SlideRocket Marketplace for purchasing related media and services including stock photography, graphic design and copy editing. See page 61.

Zoho – zoho.com

Zoho's wide range of cloud applications include its Zoho Writer word processor, Zoho Sheet spreadsheet and Zoho Show presentations package. There is also the Zoho Notepad online scrapbook application. All of these applications can be used for free. See page 54.

Photo, Video and Audio Editors

Aviary – aviary.com

Aviary offers a suite of free online media editing tools. These include a photo editor called Phoenix and its Raven vector-based drawing package, which is a bit like an on online version of Adobe Illustrator. There is also a great multi-track audio editor called Myna.

FotoFlexer – fotoflexer.com

FotoFlexer is a popular online photo editor that includes great integration with Facebook, Flickr and MySpace. See page 65.

Jaycut – jaycut.com

Jaycut is a free online video editor. It allows twin-track video editing with transitions and titles, and has direct YouTube upload functionality. See page 66.

Photoshop Express – photoshop.com

Photoshop Express is a free if very-cut-down online version of the industry-standard Photoshop photo editor. See page 63.

Pixlr – pixlr.com

Pixlr is an absolutely excellent free online photo editor. An interface called Pixlr Express is provided for image editing novices. However, for those who have experience of the full version of PhotoShop, the full Pixlr editor offers a very powerful range of tools. These include layers, a history brush and wide range of real-time filters. See page 65.

E-Mail Packages

Gmail – mail.google.com

Gmail is the very popular web-based e-mail offering from Google that provides 7Gb of storage. See page 45.

Windows Live Hotmail – mail.live.com

Windows Live Hotmail is Microsoft's online e-mail system. It offers 5Gb of storage that 'automatically increases as you need it'. See page 45.

Yahoo! Mail – mail.yahoo.com

Yahoo! Mail is an online e-mail system which claims to offer 'unlimited' storage. See page 45.

Virtual Meeting Tools

Adobe ConnectNow – adobe.com/acom/connectnow

Adobe ConnectNow is a sophisticated online application for running virtual meetings. Users can share files, notes and their entire screens, as well as using online whiteboards and audio or video conferencing. Both free and paid versions are available. See page 57.

LotusLive Meetings – lotuslive.com/meetings

LotusLive Meetings is a paid online virtual meeting tool from IBM, and one element of the broader LotusLive online collaboration suite. See page 31.

WebEx – webex.com

WebEx is a suite of online collaboration tools from Internet giant Cisco. It features file and desktop sharing combined with phone conferencing and video conferencing and is becoming an industry standard. While WebEx is a paid service, a free trial is available. See page 72.

CRM, HR, Project Management & Other Business Apps

Clarizen – clarizen.com

Clarizen provides online project management tools that can

be used to collaboratively manage anything from one-off projects to resources, timesheets, budgets or expenses. See page 71.

Employease – employease.com

Employease provides online human resource information systems that allow companies to run their payroll, benefits administration and other personnel-related IT in the cloud. See page 70.

Google Apps Marketplace – google.com/enterprise/marketplace

Google Apps Marketplace is an app store that offers a wide range of business applications that can be integrated with Google Apps (see above). Applications are provided from a wide range of vendors and cover just about every conceivable business software requirement.

Huddle – huddle.net

Huddle provides online collaboration, live conferencing, project management and document sharing tools.

Hyperoffice – hyperoffice.com

Hyperoffice is a cloud collaboration suite that provides web-based e-mail and document management, together with project management and portal tools.

Netsuite – netsuite.com

Netsuite offers a comprehensive suite of online applications for customer relationship management, accounting, enterprise resource planning, e-commerce and website management. See page 72.

ProjectManager.com – projectmanager.com

ProjectManager.com is a sophisticated online project management application that claims to be the smartest online project management software in the world. The package features a stylish graphical interface, issue tracking functions and sophisticated charting tools.

Salesforce – salesforce.com

Salesforce is a long-established provider of online sales and customer relationship management tools. See page 69.

WebEx WebOffice – weboffice.com

WebEx WebOffice is a suite of online collaboration tools that includes the WebEx online meeting application (see above), but also some very powerful tools for creating online databases, managing projects, filing expense reports and running online polls. See page 72.

Zoho – zoho.com

Zoho offers a whole host of online business applications, including the very popular Zoho Creator database application, as well as project management, recruitment, human resource, customer relationship management and invoicing software. See page 54.

Online Desktops

EyeOS – eyeos.info

EyeOS is an open source online operating system and desktop including a word processor, spreadsheet, calendar and presentation package. See page 62.

IT Farm – www.itfarm.co.uk

The IT Farm provides a browser-based version of Microsoft

Windows and Microsoft Office that runs from their online servers. See page 63.

StartForce – startforce.com

StartForce is complete online desktop with integrated word processing, spreadsheet, presentations, e-mail and media-player applications. See page 62.

Cloud Storage

Box.net – box.net

Box.net is a popular provider of online storage, with 1Gb of cloud filespace provided for free. See page 208.

CloudBerryLab – cloudberrylab.com

CloudBerryLab provide a range of consumer interfaces that allow individuals to make use of the Simple Storage Service (S3) offering that forms part of Amazon Web Services. See page 209.

Dropbox – dropbox.com

Dropbox is an online storage service coupled with a local application that automatically backs up data to the cloud and can synchronize it across multiple computers. See page 209.

Google Docs – docs.google.com

While Google Docs is an online office suite, it also allows users to upload any kind of file for online storage and sharing. 1Gb of filespace is provided for free, with each extra 20Gb costing only $5 a year. See page 48.

LiveDrive – Livedrive.com

LiveDrive provides an online storage and back-up service that claims to offer 'absolutely unlimited' online back-up for $3.95 a month. See page 209.

Simple Storage Service (S3) – *aws.amazon.com/s3*
Simple Storage Service is one element of Amazon Web Services (AWS), and provides professional, large-scale online storage for businesses. See page 99.

Windows Live Skydrive – *skydrive.live.com*
Windows Live Skydrive provides 25Gb of free online storage that can be used to back-up and share files in the cloud. See page 208.

Zoho Docs – *docs.zoho.com*
Like Google Docs, Zoho Docs offers the facility to store and share any kind of file online, with 1Gb of storage provided for free. See page 55.

Cloud Website Builders

Blogger – *blogger.com*
Blogger is a website that allows anybody to create their own blog for free.

Google Sites – *sites.google.com*
Google Sites allows anybody to easily build a public website or private intranet site with advanced functionality. Even quite sophisticated sites can be built and hosted with no payment required.

Moonfruit – *moonfruit.com*
Moonfruit is a very easy-to-use, drag-and-drop website building tool that has already been used to build over 2.5 million websites. A site with up to fifteen pages can be built and hosted for free.

Webs – webs.com

Webs is a free or paid website building tool that offers more code-savvy website designers somewhat greater technical flexibility that most of its competitors.

Wordpress – wordpress.com

Wordpress is a very popular and sophisticated tool for creating your own free or paid blogging website.

Platform as a Service (PaaS) Vendors

Force.com – Force.com

Force.com allows companies to create and run applications on the cloud infrastructure operated by Salesforce.com. See page 86.

Google App Engine – appengine.google.com

Google App Engine is online platform that can be used to develop and run applications on Google's cloud infrastructure. See page 85.

Microsoft Windows Azure – microsoft.com/windowsazure

Azure is Microsoft's platform for running Windows applications and storing data in the cloud. Customers can use the Azure platform to develop and run their online applications on Microsoft's infrastructure. See page 87.

Infrastructure as a Service (IaaS) Vendors

3Tera – 3tera.com

3Tera is a pioneering cloud computing vendor that offers a wide range of infrastructure as service configuration options.

Amazon Web Services – aws.amazon.com

Amazon Web Services (AWS) is a very popular infrastructure as a service offering. It provides a range of products including Elastic Compute Cloud (EC2) that allows processing capacity to be purchased by the hour, as well as the Simple Storage Service (S3) for commercial online storage. See page 97.

AppNexus – appnexus.com

AppNexus offers an infrastructure as a service solution that provides customers with dedicated physical servers.

Elastic Hosts – elastichosts.com

Elastic Hosts is an infrastructure as a service provider that offers cloud hosting from just 4p an hour.

GoGrid – gogrid.com

GoGrid offers cloud hosting, hybrid hosting and dedicated hosting, with the company's services generally regarded as being some of the easiest to get to grips with. See page 100.

Rackspace – rackspace.com

Rackspace is a well-known provider of traditional hosting services that now also offers a range of infrastructure as a service solutions. See page 100.

Augmented Reality

AugmentReality – augmentreality.co.uk

AugmentReality is a developer of augmented reality applications for the Layar augmented reality browser. See page 145.

Google Goggles – google.com/mobile/goggles

Google Goggles is an application for Android smartphones

that allows a picture or video to be used to conduct a visual search. See page 144.

Layar – layar.com
Layar is an augmented reality browser available for Android and Symbian smartphones and some Apple iPhones. Layar also offer a commercial augmented reality platform. See page 143.

Wikitude World Browser – www.wikitude.org
The Wikitube World Browser is an augmented reality browser available for Android and Symbian smartphones and Apple iPhones. See page 143.

Web Services

Google Checkout – checkout.google.com
Google Checkout is a web service for creating an online shop on any website. See page 34.

Google Gadgets – google.com/webmasters/gadgets
Google Gadgets is a website containing thousands of web service gadgets that can be mashed into most websites. See page 36.

Google Translate – translate.google.com
Google Translate is a website that allows text and entire websites to be translated from one language into another. Click on 'tools and resources' if you want to add Google Translate to your own website. See page 36.

Netbanx – netbanx.com
Netbanx is a payment service provider web service. See page 34.

Paypal – paypal.com
Paypal is a payment service provider web service. Click on 'Accept debit and credit cards on your website hassle-free' to learn more. See page 34.

Sitepal – sitepal.com
Sitepal is a great web service that allows you to create a 3D speaking avatar for your website. See page 36.

RBS Worldpay – rbsworldpay.com
Worldpay is a payment service provider web service. Click on 'Online payments' to learn more. See page 34.

Open Source and Open Data Resources

Data.gov.uk – data.gov.uk
Data.gov.uk is an open data resource that provides access to a wealth of UK government data for free private and commercial use. See page 224.

Fab@Home – fabathome.org
Fab@Home is an open source project dedicated to building 3D printers or 'fabricators'. See page 223.

OpenOffice – openoffice.org
OpenOffice is a completely free, open source word processing, spreadsheet and presentations package for those people who still want to install local software! See page 223.

OScar – www.theoscarproject.org
The goal of the OScar project is 'to develop a car according to Open Source principles'. See page 223.

RepRap – reprap.org
RepRap is an open source initiative for building desktop 3D printers. See page 223.

Riversimple – riversimple.com
The purpose of Riversimple is 'to provide a sustainable transport service while working systematically towards the elimination of the environmental damage caused by personal transport'. So far Riversimple has resulted in a prototype hydrogen fuel cell car. See page 223.

Fun Stuff!

Liftmagic – liftmagic.com
Liftmagic allows its visitors to upload a photograph and try out a facelift. See page 205.

OnLive – onlive.com
OnLive is an on-demand cloud gaming website that enables sophisticated 3D games to be played on any type of computer. See page 207.

Rememberthemilk – rememberthemilk.com
Rememberthemilk.com is a lovely website for creating to-do lists. See page 205.

Xtranormal – xtranormal.com
Xtranormal is a fun website that allows 3D movies to be created just by typing in words for the characters to say! See page 205.

GLOSSARY

This book inevitably uses some computer jargon. This glossary may therefore help demystify the wonderful world of cloud computing. If you cannot find the term you are looking for, try the glossary section on my **ExplainingComputers.com** website, as this is constantly updated when new terms appear.

Amazon EC2
see EC2.

Amazon Web Services (AWS)
Amazon Web Services is a popular range of infrastructure as service products. These include Elastic Compute Cloud (EC2) that provides online processing capacity, and the Simple Storage Service (S3) that allows data to be stored on Amazon's infrastructure.

Ambient computer
Ambient computers take cloud data and comfortably integrate it into the real world at the periphery of our perception. Ambient computers therefore interrupt their users far less than devices like mobile phones. Examples

include the Ambient Orb and the Ambient Umbrella from ambientdevices.com.

Android
Android is an operating system from Google. At present Android mainly runs on smartphones. However, it is already also available on some netbooks and may in future run on some tablets.

App Store
An app store – or 'application store' – is a website from which software applications are available. Such applications may either be installed on a local computing device (such as a smartphone) or integrated into a cloud service as happens when applications are obtained from Google Apps Marketplace.

Atomization
Atomization is the transformation of digital content into an atom-based, physical format that we can see, hear or touch. This means that atomization is the reverse of digitization.

Augmented reality (AR)
Augmented reality overlays data from the cloud on a real-time view of the world. For example, a user may hold up their smartphone and see arrows on the pavement directing them to the nearest tube station, or a clickable Twitter feed floating above a person's head.

AWS
see Amazon Web Services.

Azure
Azure is Microsoft's platform as a service (PaaS) offering for

developing and running Windows applications and storing data in the cloud.

Blog
A blog or 'web log' is a chronological, journal-style website maintained by an individual in the form of an online diary.

Broadband
Broadband is a high-speed means of accessing the Internet using the telephone network. Wired (landline) broadband connections use a technology known as digital subscriber line (DSL) to transmit data using frequencies not used by voice traffic. DSL is available in two variants known as ADSL (which has a slower upload speed than download speed) and SDSL (which has equal upload and download speeds). *See also* Mobile broadband.

Cloud
The Internet has traditionally been represented on network diagrams by a cloud symbol. In simple terms the cloud is therefore the Internet. However, more strictly, the cloud refers to an online computing infrastructure that facilitates the delivery of online resources including software, processing power, data storage and artificial intelligence.

Cloud as supplement
Cloud as supplement is where cloud computing resources are introduced into a business alongside traditional, in-house computing resources. For example, a company may choose to move its e-mail and office applications into the cloud, while maintaining in-house accounting, payroll and stock control systems.

Cloud computing

Cloud computing is where software applications, data storage, processing power and even artificial intelligence are accessed over the Internet from any kind of computing device.

Cloud hosting

Cloud hosting is a form of infrastructure as a service (IaaS) where customers rent virtual server instances from a cloud data centre on demand. A major supplier of this kind of service is Amazon Web Services.

Collective intelligence

Collective intelligence is captured on websites that allow the activities of one visitor to influence the information presented to another. For example, the top results in a Google or YouTube search are influenced by the content that has proved most popular with other users.

Crowdsourcing

Crowdsourcing is where the Internet is used to generate value the from activities of a great many people. Such 'pooled collective intelligence' may be contributed consciously by individuals when they use collaborative computing tools. However, crowdsourcing may also generate value by monitoring and analysing the unconscious data shadows cast by the things people consume and the objects they manipulate.

Data shadow

A data shadow is the online record or 'digital footprint' cast by a person or object whose activity is monitored in the cloud. For example, future cloud-based vision recognition systems are likely to be fed data by a great many cameras and will use this data to map a data shadow of our travels.

Dedicated hosting
Dedicated hosting is a form of infrastructure as a service (IaaS) where customers rent physical servers from a cloud data centre on demand.

Digitization
Digitization is the encoding of data, media or objects into a digital format that can then be stored and communicated in the cloud.

Diminished reality (DR)
Diminished reality refers to a potential future technology that may be able to retouch the view from our eyes in real-time in order to remove things that we do not want to see. Diminished reality technology would couple video contact lenses with powerful cloud computing vision recognition and real-time image manipulation applications.

Dongle
A dongle is a small piece of hardware that can be connected to a computer. Most usually today, dongles come in the form of a USB key that provides a 3G Internet connection using a mobile phone network. Indeed, a dongle can be thought of as a data-only mobile phone for a laptop or netbook computer.

e-Book reader
An e-book reader – or e-reader – is a mobile computing device with a high-quality e-ink screen that is primarily intended for reading books and other publications on. An example is the Amazon Kindle.

EC2
EC2 stands for Elastic Compute Cloud and is one

component of the infrastructure as a service (IaaS) product range supplied by Amazon Web Services. Specifically, EC2 allows computer processing power – or 'virtual server instances' – to be purchased on demand on an hourly basis.

Enterprise 2.0
Enterprise 2.0 refers to the use of social networking and related Web 2.0 tools within business. This may involve the use of public websites like Facebook or Twitter, or private tools like IBM's LotusLive.

Firewall
A firewall protects an individual computer or network from illegitimate external access. Firewalls can be implemented using hardware and/or software.

Google App Engine
Google App Engine is a platform as a service (PaaS) offering that allows people to develop and run online applications on Google's infrastructure.

Google Apps
Google Apps is a paid online software suite that includes Google Docs, Google's Gmail cloud-based e-mail, Google Calendar, Google Video private video hosting, and the Google Sites website building tool.

Google Apps Marketplace
Google Apps Marketplace is an app store that provides business applications that can be integrated into the Google Apps suite. For software developers, Google Apps Marketplace provides a means of distributing their cloud applications.

Google Buzz
Google Buzz is a social networking tool integrated into the Gmail cloud e-mail application.

Google Checkout
Google Checkout is a web service that enables anybody to easily add an online store to their website.

Google Chrome
Google Chrome is the name for both a web browser and a cloud operating system. Both the browser and the operating system are designed to use as few computing resources as possible, with the operating system entirely dependent on cloud applications including Google Docs. Initially at least, Google Chrome OS is only available pre-installed on netbooks.

Google Docs
Google Docs is a word processing, spreadsheet, drawing and presentations package that runs in a web browser. The application also includes an online storage facility. While anybody can register to use Google Docs for free, it also forms part of the paid, 'Productivity version' of Google Apps.

Google Gadgets
Google Gadgets is a website that features tens of thousands of web service 'gadgets' that can be integrated or 'mashed' into other websites. For web service developers, Google Gadgets provides a marketplace for distributing their wares.

Google Wave
Google Wave is a next-generation e-mail application, or as Google describe it 'an online tool for real-time

communication and collaboration'. Each Wave document can include text, images, audio and video.

GPS
GPS stands for global positioning system. Using data from GPS satellites, a mobile computing device can determine its location and report it to the cloud.

HaaS
see Hardware as a service.

Hardware as a service (HaaS)
Hardware as a service is where computer processing capacity is purchased over the web. Now a relatively old term, hardware as a service encompasses both platform as a service (PaaS) and infrastructure as a service (IaaS).

Hybrid hosting
Hybrid hosting is a form of infrastructure as a service (IaaS) where customers rent a mix of dedicated physical servers and virtual server instances from a cloud data centre on demand.

IaaS
see Infrastructure as a service.

Infrastructure as a service (IaaS)
Infrastructure as a service is the provision of online hardware on which customers can store data and run their own new or existing applications. Popular infrastructure as a service providers include Amazon Web Services (AWS), GoGrid and Rackspace.

Instance

An instance is a unit of online processing capacity, and the short term for 'virtual server instance'. *See also* Virtual server *and* Server.

Internal cloud

An internal cloud is created when a company builds its own cloud computing infrastructure to allow it to deliver browser-based software from its own data centres. Internal clouds are therefore quite distinct from the vendor-managed private clouds run by large external cloud vendors. Because internal clouds offer limited benefits, many analysts already view them as last-ditch attempts by internal IT departments to hold on to their data centres and avoid radical change. Indeed, any company with an internal cloud can be argued to not really be cloud computing at all.

Internet service provider (ISP)

An Internet service provider (ISP) offers accounts that enable individuals or organizations to connect to the Internet. Most commonly this is via a form of broadband.

Interpersonal computing (IPC)

Interpersonal computing refers to the use of the Internet to link people together and to allow them to communicate and collaborate online. Interpersonal computing often involves the use of a social networking site such as Facebook, MySpace, Ning, Bebo or LinkedIn. However, interpersonal computing may also be facilitated via collaborative software as a service (SaaS) applications.

ISP

see Internet service provider.

Layar

Layar is an augmented reality browser for smartphones. This means that it allows data from the cloud to be overlaid on a real-time view of the world.

Malware

Malware refers to spyware, viruses, keystroke readers and other categories of illegitimate software that compromise computer security.

Mashup

A mashup is a created when a number of web services are integrated or 'mashed' together to create a website that features content from many different sources. For example, a mashup may feature a YouTube video, a Twitter feed and a Google map.

Mobile broadband

Mobile broadband provides a direct wireless connection between a computer and an Internet service provider, usually using a 3G mobile phone network.

Netbook

A netbook is a small, lightweight mobile computer typically with a nine-, ten- or eleven-inch display screen and around an 80 per cent full-size keyboard. The term netbook is currently attributed to Intel (2008), although the first computers of this size and name were actually produced by Psion in the late 1990s.

Nettop

A nettop is a low-power computer usually intended to be connected to a television to enable cloud content to be accessed in our living rooms.

Office Web Apps
Office Web Apps are cut-down, online versions of Microsoft Word, Excel, PowerPoint and OneNote and one element of Office 2010.

Open data
Open data is data shared online in the public domain. For example, the UK government has made a great deal of information available for all forms of private or commercial use via a website at data.gov.uk.

Open source
Open source uses the Internet to share intellectual property and to allow the collaborative creation of things too complex to be developed by a single individual. To date, most open source initiatives have had the goal of creating free computer software. However, open source practices and philosophy are also now being applied in the creation of products as diverse as 3D printers, robots, electric and hydrogen-powered vehicles, and prosthetic limbs.

PaaS
see Platform as a service.

Payment service provider
A payment service provider or 'PSP' provides a web service for taking payments online. Examples include Paypal, Netbanx and RBS Worldpay.

Platform
A platform is a computing environment for developing and running compatible applications. For example, Microsoft Windows is currently the most common platform for running desktop software. Increasingly, however, cloud

computing developments are turning the whole Internet into a single computing platform across which online software and services can be accessed.

Platform as a service (PaaS)

Platform as a service provides a customer with cloud infrastructure and development tools that allow them to program and deliver online applications. Popular PaaS offerings include Google App Engine, Microsoft Azure and Force.com.

Private cloud

A private cloud – also known as a vendor-managed private cloud – is a very secure form of infrastructure as a service where a cloud vendor provides dedicated servers to a client organization. Infrastructure within a private cloud is never shared with other customers.

PSP

See Payment service provider.

S3

see Simple Storage Service.

SaaS

see Software as a service.

Server

A server is a computer that provides remote processing power and/or storage capacity. Servers are therefore the fundamental building blocks of cloud computing infrastructure. When rented online from an infrastructure as a service provider, servers can be real or virtual. Real servers are dedicated, individual circuit boards – known as 'blades'

– mounted within hardware racks in a data centre. Virtual servers – also known as virtual server instances – are software-controlled slices of real, physical servers. Virtual servers are created by a process called virtualization that allows many users to share the processing power of one physical server.

Silverlight
Silverlight is a Microsoft technology for displaying sophisticated media content on a website.

Simple Storage Service (S3)
Simple Storage Service is one part of Amazon Web Services (AWS). It allows customers to store data on Amazon's cloud infrastructure.

Smartphone
A smartphone is a sophisticated mobile phone with Internet connectivity that can be used to access cloud computing services. Examples include Apple iPhones, as well as phones that run the Google Android, Symbian or the Windows Phone 7 Series operating systems.

Software as a service (SaaS)
Software as a service is a computer application that is accessed over the Internet using a web browser, rather than being installed on a local computing device or in a local data centre.

Solid state disk (SSD)
A solid state disk is a storage device that saves data to memory chips rather than to a traditional, spinning hard disk.

Spyware

Spyware is a form of software – or 'malware' – used by hackers to illegitimately obtain usernames and passwords.

SSD

see Solid state disk.

Storage as a service

Storage as a service provides the facility to upload, download, share and back up any kind of data file to the cloud.

Surface computer

A surface computer is a computing device integrated into a tabletop or wall and operated via a touchscreen interface. An example is the Microsoft Surface.

Symbian

Symbian is an operating system for smartphones, such as those made by Nokia.

Tablet

A tablet is a mobile computer with a touch screen but no keyboard. Tablets are competitors to both netbooks and e-book readers for accessing cloud content. One example is Apple's iPad.

Thin client

A thin client is a networked computer that has minimal internal processing capacity. Thin clients therefore rely on computing resources supplied from the cloud or from an internal data centre.

Ubiquitous computing

Ubiquitous computing is where computing devices are built

into the real world to allow near-constant access to digital information and cloud computing resources. Ubiquitous computing is therefore the opposite of virtual reality, which is where new worlds are built within computers.

Vendor-managed private cloud
see Private cloud.

Virtual server (instance)
A virtual server – or virtual server instance – is a software-controlled slice of a real, physical server created via a process known as virtualization. *See also* Server.

Virtualization
Virtualization is the process by which dedicated, physical servers are subdivided into virtual server instances. Virtualization is one of the most fundamental technologies of cloud computing as it allows many users to share the processing power of one physical server computer. Almost all cloud computing services therefore rely on virtualization.

Web 2.0
Web 2.0 refers to the use of the Internet as a social tool and a service delivery mechanism. In practical terms this means that Web 2.0 is an umbrella term for the three key Internet developments of interpersonal computing (where two or more people communicate online), web services (where two or more websites are interlinked online), and software as a service (where people connect to online software applications).

Web service
A web service is an online gadget that can be incorporated or 'mashed' into another website to provide additional

functionality. For example, Paypal provides a web service for taking online payments, while Google provides a web service called Google Checkout for setting up an online store. Other popular web services allow maps, newsfeeds, videos, translation tools, adverts and even animated characters to be automatically mashed from one website into another.

Web Squared
Web Squared is a term coined by Tim O'Reilly and John Battelle to signal the next phase of Internet development beyond Web 2.0. The idea is that volumes of online data are going to grow exponentially – hence the squared part – as vision recognition and other sensor technologies allow more and more people and objects to cast online data shadows. In turn, these data shadows may be crowdsourced to assist in finding solutions to fundamental global problems.

Wiki
A wiki is a website that allows for collaborative document authorship. Wikis can be public, like the popular online encyclopaedia Wikipedia. However, private wikis are also increasingly popular within organizations. Private wikis can be created using free online tools including Zoho Wiki at wiki.zoho.com.

Zoho
Zoho is a provider of a wide range of online applications. These include a cloud word processor, spreadsheet, presentations package, several databases, an invoicing system, and human resource management tools.

INDEX

12seconds.tv 202
3D printing 45–8, 161, 223
3D Systems 146
3Tera 65, 244

AboutMyPlace 35
Acrobat.com 57–9, 110, 116, 156, 194, 234, 236
Adobe 57, 114, 159, 185
AI *see* artificial intelligence
Amazon 7, 11–12, 24, 97, 110, 114, 137, 148, 150, 159, 161, 162, 165, 173–4, 178
Amazon Machine Image 98
Amazon Mechanical Turk 99
Amazon Simple Storage Service *see* S3
Amazon Web Services 90, 97–100, 101, 122, 159, 174, 175, 190, 224, 245, 249
ambient computers 132, 141–3, 249
AmbientDevices.com 142–3
Android 135, 143, 144, 163, 165, 171, 176, 250
App stores 163, 173, 176–7, 250
Apple 7, 136, 138, 150, 152, 159, 161, 162, 167–8, 171–3, 174, 175, 176, 177, 178, 215
AppNexus 244
AR *see* augmented reality
Archos 136, 138, 170
artificial intelligence 22, 144, 167, 229–30
Astonishing Tribe, The 204
Asus 134, 135

Atom processor 134, 135, 138
atomization 128–9, 130, 145,
    148, 250
augmented identity 204, 213
augmented reality 21–22,
    143–5, 148, 149, 161, 176,
    185, 203–4, 205–6, 215,
    217–18, 226, 250
AugmentReality.co.uk 145, 245
Aviary 237–8
Azure 87–8, 159, 170, 215,
    244, 250

back-ups 115, 120, 121
Baidu 171
Ballmer, Steve 87, 169
Battelle, John 228–9, 230, 231
Battle for the Cloud 148, 149,
    150–78
Bebo 30, 201
BeBook 137
Bentham, Jeremy 226–7
Berners-Lee, Tim 154, 224
Bezos, Jeff 97
Big Switch, The 17, 185
Bing 35, 171
Blackberry 135
blade servers 92
Blogger 30, 32, 202, 243
blogs 32, 251
Box.net 74, 208–9, 242
Brightkite 203, 206
broadband 45, 117, 161, 165,
    251

browser wars 154
Buzzword 57, 60

Carr, Nicholas 17, 185, 186–7
Chinese government 111, 123
Chrome OS 121, 134, 138,
    163–4, 176, 177, 223, 255
Chrome web browser 45, 163,
    255
Clarizen 15, 71–2, 239
cloud 4, 7, 251
cloud adoption curve 190–1
cloud-as-supplement 189, 251
cloud celebrities 201, 209–11
cloud computing xi, 3, 4–7,
    10–11, 216, 231–4, 252
    action plan 192–7
    champions 193–4, 195–6
    characteristics 10–15
    policy 110–111, 114, 115,
        194–5
    strategy 39–41, 192–7
cloud frontiers 155–62
cloud hardware 76–103
cloud hosting 93, 95, 96–97,
    100, 252
cloud processors 219–20
cloud storage see online
    storage
CloudBerry 99, 209, 242
collective intelligence 33, 39,
    41, 222, 232, 252
computer games 201, 205–7,
    217

computing-in-the-middle 186–8, 197
ConnectNow 57, 58–9, 72, 194, 239
contact lenses 218
cost savings 16–17, 53, 183, 185, 192
crowdsourcing 21–2, 222–6, 229–31, 252
Cruise, Tom 139
CuteCircuit 141
cyberspace 127, 128, 143
cyborgs 213

data protection legislation 98, 122
data shadow 22, 214, 224–5, 229, 252
Data.gov.uk 224, 247
dedicated hosting 93, 94–6, 100, 253
dedicated physical servers 93, 94, 95, 96
desktop PCs 12, 78, 128, 132, 133, 134, 142, 152
device cloud 131–43, 147–8, 202
Digital Britain Report 117
digital cameras 132, 136, 145
digital footprint *see* data shadow
digitization 128, 130, 253
diminished reality 219, 253
direct digital manufacturing 147

dongle 117, 253
Dot Com boom 26–27
downsizing 18
Dropbox.com 74, 209, 242
Dualbook 137
dumb terminals 23

e-book readers 12, 132, 136–7, 138, 139, 173, 174, 253
EC2 11–12, 14, 15, 97–9, 100, 119, 174, 253
Eee Box 135
Eee PC 7, 134
e-ink 136–7, 139
Elastic Compute Cloud *see* EC2
ElasticHosts 245
electricity generation 17, 19, 187, 191
e-mail 5, 9, 45–7, 53, 111–12, 113, 123, 125–6, 140, 185, 197
Employease 15, 70–71, 190, 240
Enterprise 2.0 31, 254
enTourage 137
environmental savings *see* green computing
Excel 48, 59, 60, 71, 125, 169
ExplainingComputers.com i, xiii, 40, 234, 236, 249
EyeOS 62, 241
Ezarik, Justine *see* iJustine

Fab@Home 223, 247

Facebook 26, 28, 30, 39, 42, 65, 113, 123, 130, 198, 200, 202, 203, 204, 211, 212–13, 218, 224, 227, 229

Firefox 45, 223

firewall 254

First Digital Revolution 127–9, 130, 143

fixed costs 14, 159

Flickr 63, 65, 202, 208, 210

floating data centre 221–2

Force.com 86–7, 159, 183, 204, 244

Fortus 146, 147

FotoFlexer 65–6, 238

Foursquare.com 203, 205, 211

Freedom of Creation 147

Freedom of Information Act 122

Friendfeed.com 202

Friendster 30, 201

Gartner 16, 177, 188

Gates, Bill 153, 167, 171

Genentech 16–17

General Motors 218

Gmail 45, 46, 47, 52, 54, 162, 163, 202, 212, 227, 238

GoGrid 100, 119, 159, 245

Google App Engine 79, 85–6, 88, 118, 159, 165, 244, 254

Google Apps 4, 16, 46, 48, 52–4, 57, 59, 118, 163, 186, 190, 193, 236, 254

Google Apps Marketplace 163, 240, 254

Google Books 166–7

Google Buzz 47, 212, 255

Google Calendar 52, 54, 205

Google Checkout 34–5, 50, 246, 255

Google 7, 17, 24, 46–7, 54, 84, 111, 114, 115, 120, 138, 150, 155, 160, 161, 162–7, 168, 171, 175, 178, 185, 212, 215, 221, 227

Google Docs 3–4, 5, 9, 12, 28, 38, 48–52, 54, 55, 60, 61, 73, 79, 98, 110, 116, 117, 121, 125, 156, 157, 158, 163, 169, 177, 182, 193, 194, 195, 196, 208–9, 233, 234, 237, 242, 255

Google Gadgets 36, 37, 163, 246, 255

Google Gears 117

Google Goggles 144, 166, 215, 225, 245

Google Sites 52, 54, 89, 165, 195, 196, 204, 243

Google Translate 36, 162, 166, 246

Google Wave 47, 162, 255

Government Cloud 9

Gowalla 203, 206

GPS 22, 143, 203, 206, 217, 226, 256
green computing, 18–20, 97, 101, 134, 159–60, 185, 220, 221, 230, 232

HaaS 102–3, 256
hackers 9–10, 111, 121, 126
hardware as a service *see* HaaS
history of computing 151–4
Hotmail 45, 46, 227, 239
HP 138, 170
Huddle 240
HugShirt 141
Hull, Charles 146
hybrid hosting 93, 95, 96, 100, 115, 256
hybrid solutions 188–90
Hyperoffice 240

IaaS 77, 78, 79, 80, 81, 90–100, 101, 102, 103, 112, 115, 118, 159, 256
IBM 7, 24, 31, 46, 86, 89, 90, 98, 114, 150, 152, 153, 159, 160, 162, 165, 168, 174–5, 176, 178, 189, 215
iBooks 173, 174
Icelandic cold rush 19
iDisk 172
iJustine 209–10
image recognition *see* vision recognition

infrastructure 78, 90–1, 158–60
infrastructure as a service *see* IaaS
instance 257
integrated circuits 152
Intel 152, 219
intelligence 229
internal cloud 189–90, 256
International Data Corporation 107
Internet 4, 153–4
Internet-enabled appliances 132, 140–1
Internet Explorer 45, 110, 123, 154
Internet fridges 140–1
Internet service provider 9, 117, 160, 256
interpersonal computing 28–34, 35, 38, 42, 257
iPad 138, 165, 172, 173, 174, 176, 177, 215
iPhone 135, 143, 171, 172, 176, 177, 203, 206
iPod 129, 136, 138
ISP see Internet service provider
IT Farm 63, 241
iTunes 161, 173, 174, 177
iWork.com 172

Jaycut 66, 67, 238
Jobs, Steve 171

Kaboodle 203

Kindle 137, 173, 174

Klock Werks Kustom Cycles
147

laptops 12, 13, 60, 78, 109,
120, 121, 129, 132, 133–4,
138, 177

Layar 143–4, 145, 203, 215,
246, 257

Leary, Tim 30

Liftmagic.com 205, 248

LinkedIn 30, 31, 201

Linux 12, 45, 223

Livedrive.com 74, 209, 242

load balancing 91

LotusLive 31, 46, 175, 239

Macbeth 125

malware 111, 112, 113, 121,
258

mashing 35, 36, 137, 156, 202,
224

mashup 35, 229, 258

McDonald Wood, Ian 76, 77

media players 132, 136, 173

memorable account
information 113, 212

Microsoft 4, 7, 13–14, 16, 59,
84, 87, 111, 114, 124, 138,
150, 153, 155, 159, 161, 162,
167–71, 174, 176, 215, 227

Microsoft Azure see Azure

Microsoft Office 44, 48, 50,
53, 59–60, 63, 153, 156,
234

Microsoft Surface 139, 170

Microsoft Windows 41, 78,
134, 153, 163, 164, 180

Microsoft Word 9, 13, 48, 59,
60, 78, 169

Minority Report 139

mobile broadband 117, 258

mobile phones 12, 22, 23, 38,
124, 131, 132, 135, 136,
139, 141, 166, 202, 213

MobileMe 172

Moonfruit 89, 243

Mosiac 154

MySpace 28, 30, 65, 130, 201

MyTown 206

National Science Foundation
147

Naymz 202

Netbanx 34, 246

netbooks 7, 12, 43, 45, 55, 114,
121, 132, 133–4, 136, 137,
138, 142, 164, 176, 182,
258

Netscape 154

Netsuite 15, 19, 72, 240

nettops 132, 134–5, 202, 258

newspapers 137, 138

Nexus One 165

Ning 30, 201

Nokia 143

O'Reilly, Tim 27, 33, 41, 102, 228–9, 230, 231
Office Live Workspace 59–60
Office Web Apps 59–60, 110, 116, 158, 169–70, 215, 234, 237, 259
online software *see* SaaS
online storage 51–2, 60, 61, 73–4, 88, 207–9
online surveys 50, 52, 53
OnLive 207, 248
open data 223–4, 259
open source 21, 62, 222–4, 230, 259
OpenOffice 223, 247
Oracle 89, 90, 150, 174
Organovo 147
OScar 223, 247
Outlook Express 45

PaaS 69, 77, 78, 79, 80, 81–90, 101, 102, 103, 112, 159, 165, 260
PaaS vendors 84–9
Palo Alto Research Center 130
panopticon 226–8
Parviz, Babak A. 218
passwords 111, 112, 113, 123, 212
payment service provider 34, 259
Paypal 34, 69, 196, 247
Pearlman, Steve 207
Periodic Table of Videos 211

personal cloud 200–14
personal computing revolution 24, 109, 127–8, 152–3, 179–81, 184
Photoshop Express 64, 65, 238
Pixlr 65, 66, 73, 205, 238
Plastic Logic 137
platform 41–2, 78–9, 259
platform as a service *see* PaaS
PleaseRobMe.com 211
Poliakoff, Martyn 211
PowerPoint 12, 13, 48, 51, 59, 61, 169
price barrier 156–8
privacy 8–10, 47, 122–3, 201, 211–13, 214
private cloud 93, 94, 95, 96, 100, 115, 260
ProjectManager.com 240
Psion 134
PSP *see* payment service provider
PUMA 71

QUE ProReader 137
quick-wins 195–6

Rackspace 100, 118, 119, 159, 165, 245
Rangaswami, J. P. 183
Rank Xerox 130
RBS Worldpay 34, 247
Recognizr 204

Reece, George 100
reliability 116–19
RememberTheMilk.com 205, 248
RepRap 223, 248
Rightmove.co.uk 35
Riversimple 223, 248
RockYou.com 113

S3 99, 100, 101, 174, 209, 243, 261
SaaS 28, 36–38, 42, 43–75, 77, 78, 79, 81, 86, 87, 101, 102, 103, 112, 125–6, 139, 224, 261
SaaSDir.com 44
Safari 45
safe web access 112–14
Salesforce 15, 69–70, 86, 190, 242
Samsung 140
Samsung Galaxy 143
Schmidt, Eric 24
Second Digital Revolution 127–49
security 8–10, 80, 107–26
servers 90–1, 92–3, 260–1
service levels 118–19
Sidekick 124–5
Simple Storage Service see S3
single-chip cloud computer 219
Sitepal 36, 247
Skydrive 74, 120, 208–9, 243

Skytap Cloud 163
SLAs see service levels
SlideRocket 61, 237
small businesses 15, 16, 25, 54, 120
Smart Business Cloud Solutions 89
smartphones 12, 21, 22, 43, 121, 135, 143, 182, 196, 203–4, 213, 261
social networking sites 26, 30–1, 201–4
software as a service see SaaS
Solid Scape 146
Sony 136
Sony Reader 137
spyware 111, 123, 126, 262
Squidoo.com 203
Stalqer 203
StartForce 62, 63, 242
stereolithography 146
storage as a service 99, 73–4, 262
Sun Microsystems 190
surface computer 132, 139, 202, 262
Surgient, David Malcolm 13
surveillance 226–8
Symbian 143, 262
synchronous replication 120
System 360 152, 168

TabletPC 138
tablets 12, 43, 55, 132, 137,

138–9, 142, 143, 165, 170, 176, 182, 202, 262

Techno Vision 180–1

Technorati 32

Telegraph Media Group 3–4, 16

teleworking 20

thin client 135, 262

ThinDesk 20, 135

Tilera 219

T-Mobile 124

Toshiba 138

Trimmer, Dan 180

Turkle, Sherry 213

TwitPic 30, 63

Twitter 28, 30, 31, 35, 39, 41, 42, 101, 130, 198, 200, 201, 202, 203, 204, 205, 210, 211, 212, 218, 229

ubiquitous computing 128–31, 140, 263

US Airforce 175, 176, 215

US Army 151

variable costs 14–15

vendor lock-in 84

vendor-managed private cloud *see* private cloud

video editing 66, 67

video sharing 32–3

videoconferencing 59

Vimeo 32

Virginia Polytechnic Institute 141

virtual communities 26, 30

virtual reality 129–30, 143, 145, 217

virtual server instances *see* virtual servers

virtual servers 92, 93–4, 95, 96, 97–8, 100, 263

virtualization 92–3, 263

vision recognition 21, 144, 161, 204, 213, 217, 225, 228, 229

visual search 144

Wang, Charles 180

wearable computing devices 132, 141, 202

Web 2.0 27–42, 50, 65, 228, 263

Web 2.0 Summit 228, 231

web as platform 41–2

web services 28, 29, 34–6, 38, 39, 42, 264

Web Squared 228–31, 264

web strategy 39–41

WebEx 72–3, 239, 241

Webs.com 89, 244

website building tools 89

Wesch, Michael 211

Wiki 31, 264

Wikipedia 30, 31, 42, 210

Wikitude World Browser 143–4, 246

Windows Azure *see* Azure
Windows Live 59, 74
Windows Mobile 135, 170
Windows Phone 7 Series
170–1, 176
wireless network security
112–13
WordPress 32, 244
Wozniak, Steve 171

Xtranormal.com 205, 248

Yahoo! Mail 45, 46, 239
YouTube 9, 30, 32, 33, 35, 39,
40, 41, 42, 141, 144, 166,
173, 200, 202, 204, 210,
211, 217, 225, 227, 229

ZCorp 146
ZDNet 13
Zoho 15, 54–7, 67–9, 110, 116,
156, 182, 185, 194, 234,
237, 241, 264
Zoho Business 46, 57, 59
Zoho Creator 15, 57, 67–8,
88–9, 190, 204
Zoho Docs 55, 243
Zoho Invoice 69, 196
Zoho Notepad 55–7, 58, 204
Zoho Planner 205
Zoho Sheet 38, 55
Zoho Wiki 32, 194, 195
Zoho Writer 55, 60, 157, 158
Zoostorm 135
Zypad 141